Praise for *Giving Hope*

"A book of gentle wisdom, indispensable in our culture of denial, *Giving Hope* is a forthright and compassionate guide to speaking with children about death and grief in ways that support the resilience of the young soul."
—Gabor Maté, MD, author of *The Myth of Normal*

"I am so grateful for this important book, a resource that is sorely needed. We have a duty to our children to offer them a clear and genuine hope when facing the realities of death and dying. Dr. Lister and Dr. Schwartzman have given us a powerful tool to help us do that work and do it well. Jesus said, 'Let the little children come to me.' We must do no less."
—The Most Rev. Michael B. Curry, Presiding Bishop of The Episcopal Church and author of *Love Is the Way*

"Ultimately, this is a book about truth, courage, empathy, and respect for children who must learn to live with loss and their parents who must guide them."
—Steve Leder, bestselling author of *The Beauty of What Remains*

"What a gem you are holding! No less that it's about perhaps the hardest of subjects there ever was. The authors have eased what is easable, and they've held kind space for the rest. Dip in and out to suit, or read it straight through. You'll learn about the unfathomable, about the inner life of kids, about how to be there for them—and you'll learn a lot about yourself, too."
—BJ Miller, MD, coauthor of *A Beginner's Guide to the End*

"*Giving Hope* is a remarkable book by two sensitive, experienced therapists who deal brilliantly with the subject—often neglected—of how to talk with children about death."
—Clarice J. Kestenbaum, MD, Professor Emerita of Education and Training in the Division of Child and Adolescent Psychiatry and Professor of Clinical Psychiatry, Columbia University Vagelos College of Physicians and Surgeons*

"Talking with children—especially your own—about serious illness and death often feels overwhelming, but *Giving Hope* provides guidance on how to initiate these conversations. It gives parents and caregivers hope that they can help their children successfully navigate family tragedy and loss."
—David J. Schonfeld, MD, Director, National Center for School Crisis and Bereavement at Children's Hospital Los Angeles, and coauthor of *The Grieving Student*

"These authors give the incalculable gift of presence, guidance, and clarity. How to talk to siblings. How to talk to classmates and kids' friends and other parents. How to talk to the school. When the unimaginable actually happens, we need help from people who have been there and can light the way. This book, miraculously, is that help."
—**Diane E. Meier, MD, Professor, Department of Geriatrics and Palliative Medicine, Icahn School of Medicine at Mount Sinai**

"*Giving Hope* is a compassionate and practical guide for parents who need to have the hardest and the most important conversations with children, announcing and explaining death and loss. This is a book that will support adults in speaking truth and providing comfort when children need it most."
—**Perri Klass, MD, Professor of Pediatrics, New York University, and author of *The Best Medicine***

"As a pediatrician who communicates with families on difficult topics on a regular basis, I took away valuable lessons and helpful tidbits to share with families. It is a wonderful, accessible, and important read for people dealing with loss in their lives."
—**Susan Bostwick, MD, MBA, Professor of Clinical Pediatrics, Weill Cornell Medicine**

"Lister and Schwartzman's sensitive, insightful book is both practical and profound, an important guide for parents wrestling with one of their most challenging responsibilities. Enriched by poignant personal stories from decades of clinical practice, *Giving Hope* underscores the power of honesty in situations where we are inclined to hide the truth, and provides the vocabulary for the tough conversations necessary to build a foundation of trust and resilience."
—**Miguel Sancho, author of *More Than You Can Handle***

"Sharing, explaining, and comforting children in the face of losses, including death, is one of the most demanding tasks we confront. Drs. Lister and Schwartzman have created the most simple, readable, yet psychologically sophisticated guide to date. I cannot recommend this book strongly enough!"
—**David O'Halloran, PhD, Headmaster, Saint David's School**

"*Giving Hope* has the words and guidance I wish I had in my head and heart as I approached these important conversations with our children. It not only helps to make us better and more informed parents, it helps to deepen the bond between parent and child while creating a better humanity for us all."
—**Anne Williams-Isom, Esq., Former CEO, Harlem Children's Zone**

Giving Hope

Giving Hope

Conversations with Children
About Illness, Death, and Loss

Elena Lister, MD, and Michael Schwartzman, PhD

with Lindsey Tate

Avery
an imprint of Penguin Random House
New York

AVERY

an imprint of Penguin Random House LLC
penguinrandomhouse.com

Most Avery books are available at special quantity discounts for bulk purchase
for sales promotions, premiums, fund-raising, and educational needs. Special
books or book excerpts also can be created to fit specific needs. For details, write
SpecialMarkets@penguinrandomhouse.com.

Library of Congress Cataloging-in-Publication Data
Names: Lister, Elena, author. | Schwartzman, Michael, 1953– author.
Title: Giving hope: conversations with children about illness, death, and loss /
    Elena Lister, MD, and Michael Schwartzman, PhD; with Lindsey Tate.
Description: New York: Avery, [2022] | Includes bibliographical references and index.
Identifiers: LCCN 2021061855 (print) | LCCN 2021061856 (ebook) |
    ISBN 9780593419151 (hardcover) | ISBN 9780593419168 (epub)
Subjects: LCSH: Children and death. | Loss (Psychology in children). |
    Bereavement in children.
Classification: LCC BF723.D3 L57 2022 (print) | LCC BF723.D3 (ebook) |
    DDC 155.9/37—dc23/eng/20220502
LC record available at https://lccn.loc.gov/2021061855
LC ebook record available at https://lccn.loc.gov/2021061856

Printed in the United States of America
1st Printing

Book design by Shannon Nicole Plunkett

This book would never have been possible if not
for my family: Phil, Molly, Jason, Solomon, and Liza.
I dedicate this book to them and to all those
learning to live with loss.

Elena Lister

As always, for my family: Joey, Adam, Lianna, and Lisa.
And in loving memory of David Ertel, Eliot Glazer,
and Susan Sirkman.

Michael Schwartzman

For my parents, Joan and Lewis, for inspiring in
me a love of words and for always being ready
to have a conversation.

Lindsey Tate

CONTENTS

AUTHORS' NOTE

When we began writing together, we thought about the many people who have sought our help over the years. Like them, you want to talk to a child about some of life's most challenging experiences. Wherever you fall on the spectrum of loss, death, and grief, anticipated or already experienced, we wrote this book for you.

We use the word "parent" throughout for the sake of simplicity, but these pages are meant for all who take up the challenge to help a child through something hard. We thought about what would be most helpful to you and offer concrete guidance, best practices, and common pitfalls. We provide illustrative stories from our own lives and those of the people we treat, with their privacy and identities protected. We wanted to be comprehensive and tried to anticipate the kinds of questions that might arise for you.

In our work and our lives, we have seen how transformative these difficult times can be. The understandings that you can build within yourself and with your child can make even the most unbearable experiences more bearable. Whether you aim to have conversations about the concept of death itself or about past, imminent, or current losses, as you read you will see that by staying openhearted together when emotions are stirred up, you and your child can meet life's most painful realities. You will build a lifetime of connection and trust in each other, and your child can grow from your conversations, moving forward with greater compassion, more empathy, and the capacity to know and manage feelings. From your child's deepening sense of mastery in facing life's ups and downs, hopefulness is possible.

We cannot change your reality—much as we might wish we could—but our aim is for these pages to ease your way as you and your child traverse the passage through grief to hope.

Prologue

Elena's Story

"Elena and Phil Lister," I said to the receptionist, and she smiled. "They're ready for you." We were at our older daughter Molly's school, not for another dance recital or parent-teacher conference, but to talk to her classmates about death. Her little sister, our younger daughter Liza, was dying of leukemia, and we knew there were questions in the air, some asked, some not, that we felt Molly shouldn't have to navigate alone. We weren't sure what to expect.

As we entered the classroom, the third graders were filing in, shuffling, whispering, full of life, and the teachers shushed them, telling them to settle down. There were about a hundred of them filling the room, their faces turned to my husband and me at the front. Many I recognized from years of play dates and sleepovers at our house, although there had been fewer of those recently, and that was part of the problem. What did one do when the sister of a classmate was dying? Were there rules? Expectations? Liza hadn't wanted us to come in and talk to the grade; she thought it was too private. But we knew her illness was greatly impacting Molly, too, and we wanted to help with that. I scanned the room. Molly had chosen not to sit with us at the front, and there she was, surrounded by her closest friends, in one of the top rows of the tiered seating. She looked sad, scared, and brave, her arms folded across her chest. She knew what we had planned today and why we wanted to do it, as we had talked it through, but still it wouldn't be easy for her. None of it was. I felt a lump in my throat and swallowed it down, turning to Phil and taking in his loving strength.

We had sent a letter to the students' parents, explaining what was going on in our family, suggesting they talk to their child before our visit, though adding we would be prepared in case they didn't. I looked out at the children's expectant faces. Then we spoke. Briefly and to the point, explaining that Liza was sick with a disease called leukemia, that the doctors had done everything they could but the illness was too strong, that we knew that Liza would die. I said we were very sad about this, and paused. The children sat in silence, attentive, some nodding their heads. I added that even in the midst of our sadness, we were happy that we still had time left with Liza and we planned to enjoy it together to the fullest.

Next we asked the children if they had questions, or anything they'd like to say. Anything at all.

"My grandma died," a girl piped up.

"Mine, too," said another.

"I'm sorry," I said. "Did that make you sad?"

"Yes," one of the girls agreed. "She used to paint my nails."

"I almost drowned," said another child.

"And I broke my arm."

I sensed they were trying to understand, trying to match their own experiences to Liza's and Molly's to relate as best they could.

"Does it hurt?" asked a boy, his eyes wide, looking up at me.

I realized he was asking about Liza's illness, that there was empathy and compassion in his question and he hoped she wasn't in pain.

"Yes," I answered. "It does hurt. Some days are worse than others and then Liza takes medicine to make the pain go away."

I looked across the room at Molly, seeing how she was doing with all this. She had leaned forward, listening. A friend next to her had draped her arm around her shoulders. The children asked lots of questions: What did Liza do all day, what were her favorite foods, would she come back to school, did she have bandages on. And we answered them all honestly in ways the children could understand. She did have bandages but only a few. She liked to build with her Legos when she could, and play cards, look at books, and watch TV, just as they all probably did, too. We said her favorite foods were an interesting mix: Mike and Ike candy, string beans, tomatoes, watermelon, and her grandma's roast chicken. That she couldn't return to school, as she might get infections from other people, and this made her sad, but a teacher gave her lessons at our house and she did homework and was learning to read. She was determined to read before she died.

"Is she nervous?" a boy asked.

I paused. So many answers buzzed in my head. That Liza was scared of leaving us. That she was frustrated by her limitations and angry at her sick white blood cells, but was she nervous? She'd worried when things were vague about her illness, when her oncologist squirmed in the face of her pointed questions, but when he told her she wouldn't see her seventh birthday though he hoped she would make it to her sixth, her anxiety lessened. This truth, stark though it was, could be understood and processed.

I told the children some version of this. That Liza was scared and had questions, but when they were answered truthfully and talked through with me, her dad, and her sister, it helped her. It took the anxiety of not knowing away and let her see that she wasn't alone. I looked around the room at all these children with their engaged, curious faces and realized that we were going through the same process here. Creating a safe space for questions to be asked with the expectation that they would be answered truthfully. Like a game of catch where the ball is thrown, caught, and returned. A partnership. A conversation.

Phil and I had asked to come into the school to speak to the class that day. It was over twenty-five years ago and there were no formal structures in place for speaking about terminal illness and death, neither within the school system nor the healthcare system. But we needed to be there to help Molly. We'd seen her struggle to explain the situation to her friends and sensed their unease in coming to our house anymore. We had become something to be whispered about or avoided perhaps. We wanted to help the children understand a little so they would be kind to Molly and not be afraid of us. Once approached, the school was more than receptive to our wishes and helped facilitate the visit, and we were grateful for that.

Our conversation with the third graders confirmed several thoughts for me about children: they can handle the truth even on subjects that adults think are off-limits; they *want* to hear the truth; they are curious, even if fearful, around the subject of death; and having their questions validated and answered honestly creates trust. I knew this already, having seen it in my conversations with my daughters, but having witnessed this same openness in other children, this same need for the truth to address feelings of fear and anxiety, was inspiring to me. I was also struck by the children's capacity for empathy. Their attempts to equate their own illnesses and mishaps to Liza's and Molly's situations were such a heartfelt effort to understand how they might feel and to respond. They were wondering what it was like to be them. I saw that we had gone into the school to help Molly, and we did—over time many of the children showed her kindness afterward and came to the house for play dates and sleepovers as before—but our conversation had done more than that. It had helped the other children, too. They'd been given a safe space and had brought their concerns out into the open to be addressed, and they had been heard. In the back-and-forth of questions and answers, the confusion and worries they may have felt had lessened. What was vague and unknown and possibly frightening had been spoken about. This knowledge made me feel hopeful. Many parents are scared that speaking about death will terrify their children. I would suggest the opposite is true.

After Liza's death, I was determined to help others who were struggling with the illness or death of their own loved ones, taking strength from the knowledge that listening to our daughters' worries and responding to them honestly had brought them comfort and eased their anxiety. I was moved to devote my career to preventing children and adults from feeling emotionally alone when facing loss.

My involvement with schools has evolved since my husband and I visited the third grade for a couple of hours all those years ago. Since then I have put in place formal structures of support, offering frequent discussions, guidance, and follow-up to help school communities—children, parents, faculty, administration, staff—navigate illness, death, and loss together. I also work with organizations, companies, and religious institutions, guiding adults in how to convey difficult news to children. The understanding that it is beneficial for people and especially children to talk about their reactions and feelings in these situations is a wonderful sign of progress.

In my work as a therapist and grief counselor, I help my adult, adolescent, and child patients speak about all issues, including death and loss, and to learn to talk to the people in their lives about them, knowing that what is mentionable is manageable. That there is value in having conversations in order to address fears and process emotions to get through the pain to the other side, where engagement in life and connection to others is possible again. Where hope can flourish.

Michael's Story

I had always been drawn to things that scared me. Not so much monsters in the dark, but the terrors that dwelled inside. More accurately, I was moved by people who confronted and survived the monsters of emotional pain. In my early years of training as a psychologist, I chose to rotate through the pediatric oncology service at the hospital where I interned. Later I worked with college students confronting the AIDS epidemic and treated abused children in the foster care system. Through this work, I helped patients absorb, understand, and respond to crushing emotional experiences. I brought this understanding into my private practice, working closely with patients in extreme distress—a young girl whose mother died in a freak industrial accident and whose distraught father turned to me to inform and console his daughter; a parent who lost her bike-riding child when he swerved too close to the road, and was left to share the news with a surviving twin; a child who witnessed the rescue of a teenager on the brink of leaping from a bridge. I saw that illness, death, and loss wove a thread through so many people's lives.

I experienced the way talking through feelings and thoughts, making connections, bringing unconscious emotions and forgotten memories to the surface so they could be understood helped my patients feel relief from pain. I also saw how parents who could put aside their own concerns for a moment—hard though it was—in order to attend to their child's worries and fears could be the best healers for their struggling child. This became one of the most important premises of my work with children and their parents, and I carried this understanding into my work in schools.

As the first-ever consulting psychologist on staff at two of my schools, I focused on helping teachers and administrators develop a psychologically informed collective mindset to understand and address the emotional needs of students and encourage engagement with their parents on issues large and small. Over the years we weathered the TWA 800 airplane disaster, 9/11, and school shootings in the news. We confronted the illness and death of beloved teachers, parents, and even the loss of classmates. Working together, we became adept at being proactive around situations involving serious illness and death. And, most important, we believed in the benefits of talking openly with parents and students.

It was in this environment that I faced the challenge of helping the school respond to the family of one of our third graders, whose mother had late-stage melanoma and only a few months left to live. By this time, Elena was well known as a clinician with immense personal and professional experience in addressing the issues of illness, death, and loss. I was grateful to have her work closely with us to assist our third grader and his family. As she talked with parents and teachers, I found her warm and responsive, calm in such an emotional setting. We shared similar aspirations for our work within the school.

Working Together

As we met with the parents, we provided them with our best practices for speaking with their children about terminal illness and death. First, we helped them to understand and process their own reactions to the news, because we knew it would impact their subsequent conversations with their children and affect their children's own reactions. Next, we guided them in the specifics of talking to their children, the when, where, what, and how, with being honest and truthful at the top of the list. We explained the importance of being open to all possible reactions from their children as well as to their questions, and their need to hear the news more than once. We told the parents that we knew what we were asking of them was hard, and we promised we would support them each step of the way. We also said they would be surprised by their own inner strength, by what they could accomplish when they knew they had to, and by how much they would grow on this difficult journey.

We worked together for the remaining months of the mother's illness and then continued after her death, helping the community grieve together. It was a painful time for the school. The mother, a graphic designer, had been much loved, a regular presence at school events and active each year in the annual Halloween party, creating spooky signs for the haunted house. We encouraged the school to set up a memorial to her and, with the help of her husband and their son, they created an annual Halloween poster competition in her name.

As the school community moved forward, we held a final meeting with parents. We didn't have an agenda. We just wanted to provide a space for everyone to speak. Almost all the parents showed up. "I wanted to remember Regina," said one, speaking of their deceased friend. "I'll miss these gatherings," said another. "Talking everything through has been helpful." As we listened, we became aware of a general theme. The parents had been nervous about talking with their children but, when they managed to sit down with them, the conversations had gone much better than expected. When their children asked questions, they responded, as best they could, with the truth. And they handled their reactions. "Cristiano threw a book when I told him," said one. "But I took a deep breath and gave him a hug." The parents had accomplished something they couldn't have imagined and they were proud of themselves. "I didn't think I could do it. But I knew I needed to help Thomas through." They had realized the beneficial aspect of talking to their children and had put that above their own fears. "I feel closer to my son now," said a mother. "We have more of a bond." This was a refrain we heard, and not for the first time, that the parents had connected with their children on a deeper level as they'd gone through something hard together. "I really, really dreaded the conversation. But I'm glad I did it," said a father. "Really glad." A lot of parents agreed with that.

Over our many years of work as therapists, we have seen firsthand the ways in which parents struggle to talk to their children about death. They prefer not to be the harbingers of bad news, bringing upsetting information to young ears. It's a natural reaction for parents to want to protect their children from the unpleasant realities of life—we all do it—yet it's not a realistic strategy, and deep down many parents know this.

Death is inevitable and talking about death is an inevitable part of parenting. We believe it's in children's best interest to learn about death from their parents early on in their lives, to be able to have conversations about it and express emotional responses to it. We have both seen the ways in which avoiding the topic can backfire, as children learn to stifle their emotions in damaging ways that can follow them into adulthood. In our daily work, we create space for difficult emotions to be expressed and have both witnessed the sense of relief in our patients—both adults and children—as they put their hardest, most uncomfortable feelings into words and begin to realize that by talking about them they can start to handle them. We've watched this sense of mastery lead them toward hope and the possibility of finding a way to the other side of a challenging experience. Our goal in writing this book is to help you, the parent, overcome your reluctance around talking about illness and death and to encourage you to seize the opportunities that a difficult conversation brings.

In our work we have seen that a child's ability to comprehend the death of a loved one is helped immensely if he already has a realistic grasp of death in general. Our book builds on this idea and provides you with emotional support and concrete advice as you learn why and how to talk to your child about illness and death. We explain that you don't have to worry that your conversations will introduce the subject to your child before he is ready, as he is already thinking about it. All children do. Instead, you'll give his questions a place to go and allow his emotions to be expressed. He'll learn the wonderful skill of talking about—and managing—his feelings at an early age, a practice that leads to understanding other people's emotions and needs, to empathy and compassion, and to better relationships with others. We know that having this conversation with your child is not always easy, but we believe you'll be surprised by the strength you have and we'll help you to access it by being the professionals in the room with you. And we promise that talking with your child brings rewards. We've seen it. By including your child in an important discussion, you send the message that you value his thoughts and feelings and this engenders trust and strengthens his connection to you, a bond that can last even as he matures into a teenager. You'll foster resilience in him as he learns he can handle hard things and get through to where hope resides, instead of remaining mired in fear and worry. We'll help you to focus on this hope, even during the painful aftermath of death, as the knowledge that you will be able to carry on, bringing the memories of your loved one with you, can be encouraging.

In each chapter we provide you with clear guidance, key information, and actionable steps. We introduce best practices, a set of recommendations that are both appropriate and relevant for discussions in any circumstance surrounding illness or death, no matter what the specifics or context may entail. Based on our experience, these principles serve as a framework, a guiding hand, for you as you navigate your particular situation. We believe these recommendations are applicable to all kinds of discussions with children about painful topics, when adults feel anxious or challenged and may be looking for direction and support. We also draw attention to common parent pitfalls, actions that parents often take in the hope of doing what is best for their child but inadvertently make things worse. We include patient stories, scenarios, and anecdotes based on real cases and situations, and give examples of conversations and suggested dialogues. We provide answers to frequently asked questions, have highlighted key points in "takeaways," and have curated a list of further resources. By preparing you practically and emotionally as best we can, our aim is for this book to become a trusted and helpful guide.

We have consulted together on many occasions since our first meeting, and we are often struck by how the anniversaries of deaths illuminate the value of the work we do. We advise parents and children to prepare for these days, as they will commonly experience a resurgence in emotional pain. Both in schools where we have worked together and in our individual private practices, we've spoken to parents and children one year on from a death, two, five, ten years on, and seen how the ability to speak with one another about loss has been healing over time. The difficult conversations they had in the aftermath of death have helped them to cope. And they know that now. They have been able to move forward while keeping their loved one alive in their memories. There is something extremely hopeful in that.

Chapter 1

Why Is It So Hard to Deal with Death?

✳ Keeping Secrets About Death ✳ Erosion of Trust in Parents ✳
✳ The Consequences of Protecting Your Child from Difficult News ✳
✳ Cycles of Avoidance ✳ A Short History of Attitudes Toward Death ✳
✳ Talking Honestly About Death ✳

As parents, we all hope to keep our children safe as best we can and to prevent them from suffering, and, for many, this can include shielding them from news about serious illness and death. In this chapter, we'll help you to understand that this protective instinct, while coming from a good place, is not beneficial to your child and also show you why we, as a society, have reached a point where we are so uncomfortable around the subject of death.

When Brianna was eight, she was old enough to spend a month at sleepaway camp, just as her parents had done when they were her age. Over the years, she had taken in their stories of friendship and fun, and she could hardly believe it was her turn to kayak in crystal clear lakes, make hot, sticky s'mores beneath the stars, and stay up late sharing secrets with her bunkmates. She soaked up every moment, and as her camp days drew to a close, she looked forward to telling her parents all about her new experiences. When her father came to pick her up, she tumbled into his arms for a hug and he held her close, then slid her bags into the trunk. On the car ride home, she told him about fireworks that lit up the night sky and the swimming hole filled with rainbow fish, but he didn't smile in the right places or ask any questions. He didn't seem to want to listen to her stories at all and soon she gave up talking and stared out the window, wishing she could rewind time and be with her camp friends still.

When they arrived home, Brianna made her way up their front path, thinking about dinner, bath time, and sleeping in her own bed again. Her mom met her in the hallway and hugged her tight and then, through tears, said that Grandpa had died the week she had left for camp. Brianna was stunned.

"Why didn't you tell me?" she shouted.

"We didn't want to make you sad and ruin your summer," said her mom. "You'd been looking forward to camp for so long."

"It was better for you to be with your friends," said her dad.

Brianna ran through the kitchen and out into their small yard, where she clambered onto the swing. She wanted to be alone with her thoughts and, as she pumped her legs, tears streamed down her face. She could see her parents at the living room window watching her. She looked away, thinking about her grandfather, the deep laugh she wouldn't hear anymore, the chocolate bars he kept in a secret pocket in his winter coat, and the way he always let her sit in his special reclining chair when she visited. She was sad that he had died. But there was something else, a sense of loss that felt like a hole opening up inside her, a vague understanding that she'd missed out on something important. As she thought back on her days at camp, she felt guilty that she was having so much fun while her family was suffering. And she felt furious, too. With her parents, for keeping something significant from her.

Years later, when Brianna was in her teens and having a particularly difficult time in high school, she became Michael's patient. Over the weeks, as they talked, it became clear that she was still working through her anger with her parents for excluding her from her grandfather's death. In missing the funeral and the shared grief of her extended family, she felt she had mourned her grandfather alone. "I was eight years old," she told Michael. "I didn't know what I was supposed to do. I was lonely with my sadness." Even now, she was still unsure about her grandfather's cause of death or how her parents had received the news when it happened, because they had rarely talked about it. "It made my mom cry if I asked her," she said. "So I stopped asking." She shrugged. "I stopped asking about a lot of things."

Brianna felt that a rift had opened up between her and her parents, stemming from that moment. While they continued to enjoy time together, the dynamic changed. Brianna knew they had kept a big secret from her, and it had left her wondering what else they didn't think she should know. Whenever they told her something, she listened for what was missing. She started to feel she couldn't trust them to tell her the truth anymore. When she looked back on her grandfather's death, she saw it as a time of confusion in her life filled with a storm of emotions. She had turned to her parents for guidance but they seemed lost as well. As a teenager, with Michael's help, she could see that death had been the proverbial elephant in the room, that her parents hadn't known how to act or react, but as a child everything had just felt bewildering. "They didn't really mention my grandpa much after he died and nor did I. I thought that was how we were supposed to act around death—by avoiding it. It was the grown-up response and so I did that, too."

Protective Instincts Can Have Unintended Consequences

Brianna's parents had hoped to protect their young daughter from bad news and had acted with her best interests in mind. They wanted to keep death and its aftermath from intruding on her carefree summer. Their discomfort around the subject led them to hide the truth for as long as they could and then to give Brianna the news quickly, as if to lessen the blow. Afterward, the subject was closed to further discussion. It was an upsetting topic and they didn't want to make Brianna cry again or to feel sad themselves by talking about it, and so they tried to push it out of their minds. We have seen many parents of young children handle difficult news in the same protective way, as they do not want to upset their child. However, it is a classic parent pitfall, one that can have repercussions for both parent and child. Children may develop trust issues, anxiety, anger, self-doubt, and emotional inhibition, and could lose opportunities to form deep bonds with parents, or to acquire empathy and resilience. It can lead to an ongoing cycle of handling the subject of death or dying by avoiding it. As Brianna told Michael, "I clam up now the second there's any mention of death. I don't want to deal with it though I know I should."

Just like Brianna's parents, many people feel distressed about talking or even thinking about death and so they avoid it as much as they possibly can. Our aim throughout this book is to help you become comfortable around the subject, to understand the value of talking about it, and to be able to discuss it with your children.

A few years ago, Elena was asked to provide guidance in an elementary school in which one of the kindergarten teachers, Mrs. Moore, had recently learned she had terminal cancer. A beloved veteran teacher, she had shared the news with her colleagues, and they, along with the school administration, felt Elena's advice would be beneficial in navigating the difficult months ahead and would provide them with structure in supporting their friend and coworker. There was also the important question of whether to let the kindergartners know. Elena listened to the earnest discussion between the teachers and the head of school and was struck by their keen desire to do what was right for the young children in their daily care. Elena advocated telling the children the truth in a way that was appropriate for five- and six-year-olds. She believed they already had a sense that something was amiss, as their teacher was often away from school for medical treatments. Some had been direct with their questions, asking, "Why weren't you here yesterday, Mrs. Moore?" or "Mrs. Moore, how come you can't walk on your leg?" Elena thought that this sense of knowing that something was going on, but not knowing what exactly, would lead to anxiety and fear—a kind of amorphous distress—and that an honest explanation combined with guidance would lessen the students' worries.

The head of school disagreed. He believed the children were too young to deal

> **TAKEAWAY**
> Children can sense when something sad is happening with the adults in their lives and will worry less if you tell them what it is.

with the news that their teacher was going to die and was convinced that telling them would upset them prematurely. He felt they should learn the news only when absolutely necessary—after their teacher's death. In the end, the children received the explanation that Mrs. Moore was sick and that she missed school so that she could see her doctor. Elena met with the teachers to help them with their sadness and guided them on answering the children's questions. As Mrs. Moore's illness progressed and she lost her hair and her energy, the children were not told that she would die. The head of school still thought it best to keep the news secret and banned parents, caregivers, and staff from discussing the inevitable death with the kindergartners. When Mrs. Moore left the school for good, the children were not informed that she would not return, and when she died a few months later, they were blindsided and distraught. An uncomfortable feeling that information had been kept from them compounded their grief, but they didn't know how to address it. They didn't have the words to articulate all the emotions roiling inside them, and they learned from the adults in their lives that death is something that people sidestep, prefer not to mention, and tend to avoid in conversations. And so they pushed everything they were feeling deep inside, but it manifested in other ways through their behavior—temper tantrums, sulking, bouts of crying, bedwetting, clinginess, separation anxiety, fear of monsters—both at home and at school for a considerable length of time.

While Elena was able to help the children with their grief, offering them time and space to talk about missing Mrs. Moore through art projects and a goodbye ceremony, it is likely that this early encounter with death, without available preparation, will stay with the children, potentially impacting them on many levels, and causing them to feel unease around illness, death, and dying throughout their lives. Their school's good-hearted attempt to shelter them from bad news did not work. Instead they suffered a double loss: that of their

teacher as well as an intangi-
ble loss of trust in the adults
they relied on to guide them.
It's easy for parents to fall into
a similar trap.

Throughout our book, we
share best practices to help
you avoid common pitfalls

TAKEAWAY

Trying to shield children
from news about a death
can lead to a loss of trust in
your honesty.

---

when illness, death, and loss enter your life. Some of you may feel
worried that you have already handled a death by avoiding it and
have seen your children struggle as a result, or are concerned that
you may do so in the future. Our response is that, while we believe
we all carry our past experiences with us, especially difficult ones,
we know through our work that we can learn to look at them anew
and alter the ways they affect us. The good news is that there are opportunities for you as parents—and for your children—throughout
your lives to lessen the impact of past traumas. That it is always
possible to revisit and reconsider prior losses.

Why We Feel Uneasy Around Death—a Historical Perspective

You are not alone in feeling uncomfortable around death. There are
myriad reasons why so many of us—especially in Western society—
find the concept of death alarming and the idea of having an everyday conversation about it intimidating. It is not an individual failing
or a character flaw.

As little as one hundred years ago, people used to have a much
more tangible and immediate experience with death and dying,
as it was common for people to die at home, surrounded by family, friends, and even members of the local community. In villages,
church bells tolled to announce a death to all. Often the body of

the deceased was laid out in an open casket in the front room for everyone to pay their last respects, and many larger houses had a designated "death door" through which the body was carried for burial. From a very young age, people were aware of the reality of death. They had probably experienced the death of a family member, gathered with others at someone's deathbed, and would have expected to die in a similar way. Death was a natural part of the life cycle.

By the twenty-first century, prior to the coronavirus pandemic, things had changed dramatically and, for many, death was swept to the edges of our vision. This reluctance to confront its reality was brought on over the past fifty years or so, as the majority of us lost touch with the physical experience of death.

Advances in medicine and innovations in medical technology provided the means for people to live longer, and so we experienced fewer early and unexpected deaths

> **TAKEAWAY**
> You may feel uncomfortable talking about death because our society as well as the generation that raised you didn't show you how.

among our loved ones. People survived once-fatal illnesses and life-support equipment bought time for desperately sick patients, allowing their bodies to overcome critical illness. In this way, death became thought of as the province of the very old and we reacted with shock to news of anyone who died too young, which in some cases could mean before they reached their eighties.

These same advances in medicine ensured that when people died, they often did so in hospitals where they had gone to seek life-extending treatment, in nursing homes where around-the-clock care helped them navigate chronic and debilitating diseases of old age, or in hospices. In many cases, they died far from home, often out of sight of their family and friends, the communal deathbed very much a thing of the past. It was hardly a surprise, then, that many of us felt out of our depth around death. For the most part, we had little direct experience ourselves and we rarely had adults in our lives who modeled expected behaviors and protocols. The more unfamiliar death became, the scarier it seemed, fostering our wish not to think or talk about the subject. It made sense that our natural instinct was to try to ignore it as best we could.

Some would argue that the coronavirus pandemic changed all that, that finally we were forced to confront the existence of death. Certainly, we were brought face-to-face with our own mortality, and many millions of people lost a loved one to COVID-19 around the world. However, our experience has shown us that most of us have not become more at ease in dealing with loss or speaking about it—just as those who live through war or with daily neighborhood violence are not necessarily more comfortable with the subject. We became overwhelmed when thinking about death, or oversaturated and inured to it. We felt unsafe and afraid, and some of us turned into experts in avoidance.

Rather than bring us closer to the physical reality of death, the pandemic, through social distancing protocols around travel and hospital visits, caused many hundreds of thousands of people to endure the death of a loved one from a distance, unable to say goodbye in person or to grieve afterward as a community. Researchers have shown that for each person who died due to COVID-19, nine family members were affected by that loss. That's millions of people grieving in this country alone. Others were overwhelmed by deaths of loved ones combined with generalized stress—job loss, financial insecurity, fear of illness, loss of routine—caused by the pandemic. When there is just too much to cope with, people steer clear of distressing subjects. Mass exposure to death or serious illness does not make one better at dealing with it, nor does it make personal loss easier. Paradoxically, the pandemic may have exacerbated our avoidance of talking about death as a society.

For many parents, death remains as taboo a subject as ever, morose and macabre, dodged as much as possible, talked about little. It's not exactly welcome dinner-table conversation and it's really not something to talk about with, or even in front of, the children. Just as we may be fatigued by the subject of death, now we might even think, "They've heard so much about it already. They're so young. Let's not add to their burden."

We recognize why parents might choose avoidance instead of confrontation when it comes to conversations about illness, death, and loss. So many parents we know have said to us, "Really? Do I have to talk about it?" Our answer is yes. Evasion may seem easier but it will affect your children adversely and, potentially, for years to come. The simple and difficult truth is that ignoring the subject does not make it go away.

A few years ago, Elena was asked to help out in another school in which a kindergarten teacher was navigating a terminal illness. She advocated for telling the children, and this time the school considered her advice and agreed to proceed. With Elena's encouragement and the headmistress's backing, Mr. Morales, the teacher, took a brave step and made a video for his class, telling them he had a big, big sickness that the doctors weren't able to fix, and that he did not have long to live. He explained that he was going to leave the hospital and go home to be with his wife, and that doctors and nurses would care for him there until he died. He added that he knew the children were in good hands with their new teacher, Ms. Jordan, and that he was proud of them all.

The plan was for the kindergarten parents to show the video to their child after school on a certain day, and Elena met with them all to help them navigate the process. She knew it was going to be difficult for them. Many had already expressed concern. Some had said they didn't think they should, or didn't think they could. Elena listened to their fears and gently explained that it was best for their children, as they had already suspected that something was wrong. She described that knowing in advance would help the children, that the opportunity to show their appreciation to Mr. Morales, and the process of saying goodbye, would make it easier for them when he died. She promised to be available to them for support. "It's okay for you to be sad," said Elena. "It's okay for your child to cry, or to say nothing at all." She had provided guidelines for the parents beforehand, explaining the importance of letting each child know what was going on. She had developed a plan with the school, and at its core was the need to address the facts, no matter how sad they were, and present them to the students in a way that would help them to understand and be involved with this important event. Sharing the video was the first step.

The next morning, the children met as a class with their teachers and discussed the video. Some of them cried, some sat in silence, and some had a lot to say. "I want Mr. Morales here," said Savannah. "He's our teacher. I miss him." "Why can't the doctors fix him?" asked Zoe. The teachers were prepared for questions and answered them honestly. Next, they offered each child the opportunity to make a card for Mr. Morales so he would know they were thinking about him and wishing him well. For the rest of the morning, the children worked on their creations, and, by lunchtime, their bright cards were in an envelope ready to be sent to the hospital. Then it was time for science. It was important that the children go about their usual routines.

The next Friday, the children sang their favorite songs and a video was sent to Mr. Morales at home. The following week they painted pictures of the storm that had blanketed everywhere in snow, a big stack of cheerful snowmen and snowball fights. "This is you," wrote

Sam at the bottom of his picture of a man in a red hat on a sled. Mr. Morales lived for seven weeks after he left the hospital, and each week the children worked on a project for him. It became part of their school routine.

After his death, a school assembly was held and the kindergartners filed in. They sang "Twinkle, Twinkle, Little Star" in Spanish, just as Mr. Morales had taught them when they first started in his class. The headmistress lit a candle and asked for a minute's silence, and, astonishingly, the children were quiet, 50 five-year-olds remembering their teacher.

While the children were understandably deeply saddened by Mr. Morales's death, they were able to process it and move forward with their grief. They knew that they could talk about him, that nothing had to be kept hidden away or avoided. They felt good that they were able to show him how much they cared about him, before it was too late. To our knowledge, there were almost no instances of behavioral problems. At each step of this journey, Elena had guided the adults to face the death in an open and honest way and they had managed extraordinarily difficult things. Mr. Morales addressed his own mortality directly; the parents shared the video, though in many cases it was far beyond their comfort zone; the teachers stayed open to the children's feelings or questions while continuing with their school routine. In each case, the adults focused on the children's needs and reactions, and responded empathically. With all these careful measures in place, the children were given a gift: a sense of greater ease in handling serious illness and death, one that they could take forward and use as they grew older.

Our aim is to help you to see how such an open dialogue can benefit your child when you need to speak with her about illness and death, and to provide you with the tools—and the confidence—to guide her through a difficult situation, no matter your particular circumstance.

Chapter 2

The Case for Talking with Your Child About Death

✻ Talking Helps Both You and Your Child ✻

✻ Children Think like Scientists ✻

✻ Your Child Already Knows About Death ✻

✻ The Need for Parental Guidance ✻ When Your Child Worries Alone ✻

✻ Tending to Your Child's Reactions ✻ The Importance of Empathy ✻

✻ Facing Your Uncertainty—to Help Your Child ✻

✻ Hard Conversations Lead to Deep Bonds ✻ Fostering Resilience ✻

Though we may wish it were not so, death is an inescapable part of childhood. It might come in the form of the loss of someone close, a member of a child's community, or within the larger world, the news delivered via the media. However it arrives in your child's life, it will ensure that dealing with death is an unavoidable part of parenting. In our work, we have seen that many parents accept this undeniable truth and yet they are still reluctant to take the steps to have conversations about death with their children. They tell us they are scared they will damage their child in some way, or that they worry about handling their child's reactions. They may fear their own feelings around death. In many cases, parents consider themselves ill-equipped to have such an important conversation and, in their worry over doing a good job, they may say nothing at all. Perhaps you have experienced this paralysis yourself. We recognize that the reasons for inaction are rooted deep within, a combination of personal experience with loss and pervasive societal discomfort, and, as we discussed in Chapter 1, often come from a place of fierce love. We believe, however, that speaking about death is beneficial to children and parents alike. We are here to help you through and to tell you it's okay to start small, to revisit, to get it wrong, but ultimately our experience has taught us that talking is the best way forward.

There are different situations in which you may find yourself wanting to avoid a conversation about illness or death. Your child might bring it up out of the blue—perhaps she's seen a TV show in which one of the characters gets sick or dies—and have general questions surrounding death. Another is when a specific death has occurred that will impact your child's world. We understand that these are very different conversations, and that telling your child about the loss of a loved one may bring with it an extraordinary amount of emotional pain for all involved. We would say, however, that our statement remains true for whatever situation you may encounter. Talking will help both you and your child.

Why You Might Not Want to Talk About Death

Let's consider the primary concerns that prevent parents from engaging with their children in conversations about illness or death.

Parents Worry That They Will Introduce the Subject and Cause Their Children to Have a Scary View of the World

We have found this is a very common fear. Parents hope to provide a happy childhood for their child, one filled with simple joys and as far removed as possible from the stressors of the adult world that they will enter all too soon. They wish to keep the troubling presence of serious illness and death at bay if they can. Ultimately, it is a fruitless battle, as children are surrounded by death in their daily lives—and are fascinated by it. They observe the life cycle of plants and trees in their own backyards or in city parks, and accept that leaves and flowers grow, bloom, wither, and die. They notice a dead worm on a sidewalk and comment that it is not moving, or they see a car-flattened pigeon and feel sad. This interest in the world around them leads to a growing awareness of the concepts of life and death.

Some children are exposed to death in their families or communities and may overhear fragments of adult conversations, either spoken about when a child is presumed far away or mentioned directly in front of a child considered too young to understand. Other children hear announcements about death from the news or on their parents' TV shows. Or they come across death in fairy tales, children's books, TV series, and movies. They don't have to look far to find references to it, and these inklings will start to fit together to build their jigsaw of understanding.

You need not feel concerned about your child learning that death occurs. It may be helpful for you to know that even at the young age of three or four, children are seeking to understand death just as they do so with anything else that makes them curious. Children think like scientists. They gradually gather their observations into a theory in order to make sense of the world around them. Between the ages of three and ten, they develop an understanding of four important elements of death: its universality (all living things die), its irreversibility (death is permanent), its finality (all functioning stops), and its causality (death occurs for different reasons)—we expand on these concepts in Chapter 4. They will not comprehend all the steps at the same time, and each child will learn the fundamentals according to his own timetable. Sometimes they will seem to know and not know at the same time. The young daughter of a friend of Michael's liked to rewatch the movie *Bambi*, and each time the opening scenes played, she announced with great joy, "Look! Bambi's mother's alive again!" She knew that death was permanent and yet couldn't stop herself from hoping that it was reversible, too.

Children absorb information from their surroundings, but they also need parental guidance as they figure things out about the world. The subject of death and dying is no exception. It may seem terrible to have to discuss such a somber subject with your child, and yet by not saying anything you are sending the message that death is something that shouldn't be mentioned. Instead, if your child is curious about death and you talk about it with him, he is likely to accept it as part of the big world he is exploring. If your child's life has been impacted by the death of someone close to him, your ability to discuss it with him will help him to weather the storm. The more you are able to engage with your child and talk about death as natural, the more comfortable your child will be around the subject. In later chapters, we will expand on best practices for having these conversations.

Parents Believe They Will Make Their Children Fear That People They Love Might Die

Children become aware of death whether a parent introduces them to the concept or not, and it is true that they may connect their burgeoning knowledge to the idea that people they love may die. This is a reality that many parents find hard to face, as they dislike the idea of their child feeling sad and scared—or contemplating being left alone after a parent's death. It is common for parents to be caught off guard when their small child asks, "Is Grandpa going to die?" or "Are you going to die?" and they may deflect the question or brush it off, leaving their child confused and anxious.

One of Elena's patients, an intelligent and lively five-year-old girl named Emily, questioned her on what happens when people die. Elena's response was to ask Emily how her parents had responded to the question. Emily wriggled in her chair. "I don't know," she said. "They don't talk about stuff like that."

It turned out that Emily's aunt had died recently and when her parents gave her the news, she asked if they might die, too. They seemed upset and angry about her question and told her they were fine. When she asked them again, they changed the subject. But Emily had questions still, and without an outlet for them they churned in her mind, woke her up in the middle of the night, and sent her running to her parents' bedroom. It had reached the point that she dreaded falling asleep and couldn't go to sleep alone. At this point, Emily's parents had sought Elena's help with her behavior.

Just as no one really likes to talk about death, we especially do not like to talk about our own deaths, but when children ask these questions it's important to be able to answer them. Emily's parents fell prey to a classic parent pitfall. By saying they were fine, they hoped to allay their daughter's fears and stop her from worrying. They thought that dwelling on the subject of death, especially their own deaths, would frighten her more and they decided it was best not to engage further on the topic. But avoidance can create mis-understanding and without the ability to ask a parent and receive honest answers to questions, a child may stifle her curios-ity, build an unhealthy fear of the unknown, and develop overwhelming anxiety, as Em-ily did.

TAKEAWAY
Since children will think about death, it is better to have that thinking be with your guidance rather than on their own.

With guidance from Elena, Emily's parents began to un-derstand that their daugh-ter's struggles at bedtime stemmed from her worry about them dying, and that not being able to talk about her fears with them had exacerbated the problem and not protected her at all. They learned how to answer Emily's questions in ways that felt com-fortable to them and reassured her, and her dread of bedtime has since receded.

Children do not have a store of prior experiences and knowl-edge about the world to help them with what is unknown. To them it can be terrifying. They need guidance to define, understand, and manage it. Though it may seem counterintuitive at first, children will not be traumatized by speaking about the death of loved ones, as it is something they are already thinking about alone—instead they will feel relief in being able to ask questions, air their worries, and hand over their anxieties to a caring adult. Emily now knows that when she reaches out to her parents, she will be heard and they will answer her queries as best they can.

Parents Are Concerned That They Are Ill-Equipped to Handle Their Child's Reactions and Do Not Want to Feel Helpless amid Their Child's Distress

We hear frequently from parents that when they are building up to telling their children about illness or death, they play out different scenarios in their mind. In these scenes, their child responds with a torrent of intense emotion or a bewildering silence and this reaction pulls the parent up short, stopping them from proceeding with the conversation. The fear of having to handle a child's reaction is real, as children may well feel upset, scared, or even angry on hearing about death. However, while it may be tempting to avoid a conversation in an attempt to prevent the onset of these reactions, this strategy is a temporary fix at best, one that protects the parent but not the child. We have already seen that children are aware of death around them even when a parent hasn't talked to them about it, and that they also are perceptive enough to sense when something important is being kept from them, and so they will likely experience strong emotions anyway. It's much less overwhelming for a child to process these feelings with a parent instead of having to deal with them alone.

Young children have strong feelings about lots of things—starting school, a new sibling, changes in routine, broccoli for dinner—and they can express their reactions in many different ways. Seeing your child in distress can be hard to witness, especially if you are struggling with the news of a death or illness yourself, but being able to help your child regulate her emotions—and to manage your own when confronted by hers—is an important part of parenting. A child may sob on hearing about the death of someone she loves, withdraw into sadness, or feel something in between. This is natural behavior—these are emotions that people young and old express when someone they love is seriously ill or has died, but they may be new for your child. She will look to you for guidance. If you can see these moments as an opportunity to tend to your child in a useful way rather than focusing on your own response to her reactions, you will feel more able to cope.

It may help you to know that you have been navigating this terrain and attuning yourself to your child from the very first moment you met her. Your tone of voice, your eye contact, and the words you use to engage with her forge an emotional connection and support her growth toward independence. When you help her with her first steps ("Look at you walking!") or see her stumble ("You're okay"), she notices your understanding and absorbs it. Over time, as she experiences your trust in her, she comes to trust herself, developing into her own person, perhaps going off to kindergarten or riding a bike. As you encourage her independence with words, she turns your belief in her into "I can do this!" Your attunement to your child, this flow of emotional currents between you, lies at the heart of your bond with her and will help you enormously as you navigate talking to her about something upsetting.

When your child reacts to news of a death, if you can relate to her feelings in order to meet her needs, you will help her gain a sense of mastery in the face of something confusing and difficult. As she experiences you comprehending her, she will see that something that seems unbearable and overwhelming can be understood and tolerated and that together you will make it through. In later chapters we provide you with specific guidance to give you more confidence in handling your child's reactions, whatever they are, in ways that continue to build a bridge between you and enable her to cope with her own emotions as she grows up.

Parents Are Reluctant to Deal with the Feelings That Conversations About Death Can Bring Up for Themselves

Talking about death inevitably stirs up our own thoughts, fears, and memories around the subject—especially the recollections of deaths of loved ones and the anticipatory anxiety around our own mortality. Often parents try to avoid these feelings of discomfort, but in doing so they can unintentionally transfer their worry to their children, who will sense it and take it on as their own.

Six-year-old Adam is one of Michael's patients. Until recently he was a happy-go-lucky first grader, embracing his growing independence. Even when the coronavirus pandemic changed his life dramatically, he coped well, attending classes online and seeing friends through the computer screen. However, after a few months he started to become anxious every time his mom went downstairs or when she walked down their driveway to collect the mail. He became clingy and needed to hear her making noise nearby when he was falling asleep at night.

"It's so unlike him," his mom, Kayla, told Michael when she sought his help. Michael asked whether she thought Adam's fears might be related to the coronavirus, and she said he seemed to be fine. She didn't let him watch reports of it on television and always monitored his time online so he wasn't saturating himself in information about it.

"How are you doing with everything yourself?" Michael asked, and Kayla's eyes filled with tears.

"It's hard," she said. "I'm scared we'll catch it and end up in the hospital."

Michael learned that Kayla kept tabs on her son constantly, checking him for symptoms, taking his temperature. As they talked, she told Michael that her father had died in the intensive care unit when she was a teenager and she still remembered being frightened by all the tubes attached to his body. She had kept her fears to herself, not wanting to burden her mom, who was struggling with the decision to withdraw life support. Kayla didn't want Adam to go through the same thing, and she hadn't been able to answer any of his questions about COVID because it brought back all her unprocessed memories.

It became clear that Adam had absorbed his mother's anxiety. As soon as he understood that he could tell Michael anything he wanted, he was able to share his fear that his mother would die, a huge relief for him. Over several weeks, Michael helped Kayla see how her worries about illness and loss were being conveyed indirectly to her son. She came to understand that addressing her own anxiety first and then talking with Adam would be helpful for both of them.

In the next chapter, we coach parents to open themselves up to exploring their own feelings and reactions to death so they can "clear their own noise" and ground themselves before turning their attention to their child. This frees them up to be more attuned to their child's needs as they talk to them about death.

Parents Realize It's an Important Conversation and Don't Want to Mishandle It

While death is always around us if we look, the coronavirus pandemic immersed us all in a soup of mortality. We have seen an uptick in parents reaching out to us as they and/or their children struggle with the cumulative assaults on their mental health brought on by coping with uncertainty, the loss of life as they know it, the constant engagement with death, and, for some, grief over the death of people they love. Very often, parents explain to us that they know they should be having conversations about death with their children but they feel overwhelmed or underprepared. They don't know where or how to begin and so they promise themselves they'll look into it and set aside time next weekend. But still they don't. They feel unsure. We would agree that talking about illness and death is probably one of the most important conversations you can have. However, we would suggest that this should not stop you from having the conversation; instead it should make you more determined to do so. We hear parents saying, "I didn't know what to say so I thought it best to not say anything," or "I didn't want to ruin my son for life by getting it wrong." We would like you to know that you should not overthink a conversation or look on it as a make-or-break moment. It need not be perfect. It does not have to happen all at once and it does not have to be long, but it is in the best interests of your children to have one. It can be readdressed another time if you think you have mishandled it the first time, modeling to your children that you may ponder what you've said and find ways to amend it. You might say something like, "I'm sorry, I didn't say that the way I wished," or "I'd like to add to what I said." Perhaps knowing that this is a conversation that you will return to and add to over time as you and your children develop will take the pressure off.

TAKEAWAY

An initial conversation about death with your child does not need to be perfect. You can always revisit the subject.

There are many positive reasons for speaking with your child about death, and one of the most compelling is the act of having a conversation itself. When we talk with parents, we are often struck by the care that lies at the heart of their reluctance to tell unsettling news to their children, by their urge to protect that stops them from speaking. We encourage you to see that having a difficult conversation with your child is a way of showing kindness. When you feel brave enough to share upsetting news and are responsive to your child's needs, staying with him through his reactions, you are modeling empathy and showing him that you care. This back-and-forth of words and emotions engenders trust, solidifies a parent-child connection, and sends the message that you have the time and inclination to include your child in important matters. Parents often try to shield children from what they consider grown-up conversations with words like, "You don't have to worry about this now." We've seen that parents mean well when they say this, but instead these words send the message that parents aren't open to talking about everything with their child, that maybe they aren't being truthful, or perhaps they don't trust the child with the truth. A child who learns that his questions will not be answered by his parent is likely to find perhaps incorrect answers elsewhere, from his friends or online.

In contrast, when your child sees you caring enough to be honest with him on such a significant topic, he will trust you to be truthful in the future and continue to turn to you with worries, concerns, and problems, even as he matures into a teenager, when burgeoning independence can raise challenging topics. When you sit with your child and help him navigate tough situations by talking them through, instead of avoiding them, it teaches him that you believe he can process and handle them. This, in turn, helps him foster resilience. He sees that you can both get through hard things together and this gives him confidence for the next challenge. The trusting bond formed by open conversations on difficult topics lays a foundation for life.

TAKEAWAY

If you talk with your child about death, you can modulate what you convey rather than his going elsewhere with his questions and getting answers in a less caring and planned setting.

Chapter 3

Know Your Own Thoughts and Feelings About Illness and Loss

Introducing Best Practice:
Know your own thoughts and feelings

❋ Your Thinking Impacts Talking with Your Child ❋
❋ Taking Care of Your Needs First ❋ Leaving Your "Baggage" Behind ❋
❋ Turning Inward to Tune In to Your Child ❋ Questions to Ask Yourself ❋
❋ Reflection Can Bring Relief ❋

Often as parents, when we think about talking with our children about a difficult subject such as death, we are so focused on doing what is right for them that we forget how *we* factor into the equation. When speaking with children we are not just conveying information—we are impacted by the situation, too, and our thoughts and feelings will affect the conversation. This chapter addresses one of our best practices: *Know your own thoughts and feelings.* Here, we'll give you precise guidelines to enable you to tune in to your own emotions first to better understand and help yourself and, in turn, to be more equipped to tend to your child as she hears and processes the news of a death.

One of Elena's patients, Russ, had planned to tell his two children, aged four and six, that his father—their grandfather—was ill, and to help them understand that Gramps would have less energy than they were used to and would probably have to rest more.

"It was a disaster," said Russ, shaking his head. "I sat the kids down and told them I had some sad news, and then I lost it. I couldn't stop crying, couldn't get the words out. I just said, 'Sorry, we'll talk later.'" He rubbed his hands over his face and reached for the tissues. "What are they going to think?"

"Maybe that their father is very, very sad," said Elena. "That's rough that it didn't go as you hoped, but that happens to all of us sometimes. Did Mia and Jaden say anything?"

"Mia was silent, just looked at me with her big eyes, and Jaden patted my hand."

"What about Michelle? Was she there?"

"She had to work late," said Russ. "I should have waited, but I thought I would be fine. I mean, he's not dying. The strange thing is, I wasn't upset about my dad. I found myself thinking about my mom. She died suddenly when I was in college and . . ." He stifled a sob and took a deep breath. "I never got to tell her how much I loved her or what a great mom she was." Tears streamed down his face. "I feel grateful I've been able to express my gratitude to my dad and that Michelle and the kids can, too. Before it's too late."

As Russ and Elena talked, it became clear that he had never really let himself process his mother's death. He had pushed thoughts of her away each time they surfaced, as they brought overwhelming feelings of sadness and guilt. With Elena's gentle questions, he remembered her.

"She would have been so proud that my dream to have my own store came true," he said quietly.

Elena nodded. They sat for a few moments.

"Should we talk about revisiting your conversation with Mia and Jaden? They'll want to know why their dad was so sad."

Russ agreed. That was very important, too. He realized that while it still might not be easy for him, he felt more able to speak with them now that he understood better the root of his sorrow.

In the best-case scenario, you will have the chance to speak with your child about the concept of death in general before the need arises to talk about a specific serious illness or death of someone close (and in the next chapter we'll elaborate on ways to do this). However, no matter the situation, before talking to your child about death of any kind, we recommend that you take the time to recognize your own feelings first, as your conversation will have a multidimensional aspect to it. Your thinking will be informed by all your past experiences with illness and loss, your own concepts of death, and how you anticipate your child will react—as well as how you might respond to that. It is easy to see why there is huge potential for emotions to ignite and flare, and for a conversation to go down an unpredictable path. For Russ, unexpected memories of his mother's death made it challenging for him to talk with his children about his father's deteriorating health. Just as a flight attendant instructs airline passengers to put on their own oxygen mask before assisting others, we advocate that parents take care of their own needs first by giving time and thought to unprocessed feelings.

Melanie, a friend of Michael's, called him one lunchtime, so overwhelmed with sadness that he could barely make out what she was saying. After a few minutes, he determined that her beloved dog had died and that she had no idea how she would tell her children when they came home from school later in the day.

"They'll be just devastated," she said. "They love Riley so much."

Michael offered to go for a walk with Melanie to help her gather her thoughts, and as they wandered through the park she told him about Riley. The way she brought a different gift to each person that arrived at the house and how she could hear the refrigerator door open from two rooms away.

"Was she your first dog?" asked Michael.

Melanie shook her head. Her first dog, Smudge, had died when she was six but her parents had not told her. Instead, she had arrived home from school one day to find a new puppy waiting in the kitchen. She loved this new bundle of fun but she wondered about Smudge. "He went to live with a friend in the country," said her dad. "He's happy there," said her mom. "Bounding through long grass and chasing rabbits." Melanie pictured him in her mind and thought that sounded fun. She missed Smudge very much but she loved the new puppy, Birdie, and eventually she stopped asking questions. Later, when Birdie grew old and died while Melanie was in college, her parents had brought home a new puppy within a couple of days. She understood then that they were trying to escape feelings of sadness and had papered over their loss with the frolics and distraction of a new puppy. Finally Melanie realized that her parents must have done the same thing with Smudge, replacing him when he had died without telling her. When she asked them about it, they admitted the truth.

Now with Riley's death and the need to be honest with her own children, she was hit afresh with an onslaught of emotions about the loss of Smudge. It had been her first experience with death and she had never had the opportunity to grapple with the reality of it, to face emotional pain and make her way through with the guidance of her parents. They were too busy avoiding reality. She was tempted by the idea of doing what they had done and giving her children a new dog to distract them from their own hurt. Instead, with Michael's encouragement, she hoped to find the strength to face the loss herself and to help her kids navigate their pain. She gave herself over to her memories, remembering Riley, Smudge, and Birdie.

Later that afternoon, Melanie was able to tell her children the terrible news, to sit with them as they took in her words, and to cry with them. As she looked at their faces, turned toward her for guidance, she realized if she had not taken the time to recognize how her own reaction to the death was layered and heightened by her past experiences, she would have brought the weight of it all to this interaction. Instead, she was able to focus on her children and what Riley's death meant to them. It was their first experience of personal loss—and that was big enough for them to handle without her additional "baggage."

> **TAKEAWAY**
>
> Processing your own feelings first helps you to be able to focus on your child.

Over the next days and weeks, Melanie began to see how her first experience with death as a child had impacted her reactions to other losses she had suffered during her childhood. She had felt numb after the death of each of her grandparents and again when a friend died in a car accident during college. She realized now it was as if she hadn't been able to deal with the reality of the deaths, or the pain that each one brought, and so she had hidden her thoughts and feelings away. Only with Riley's death—and the need to address it for the sake of her children—was she able to go back in time, start to process each death, and begin to grieve.

The death of a loved one can bring on intense feelings as well as the need to handle practical elements—speaking with relatives, arrangements for burial or funeral rites, juggling work and childcare—and demands on time and emotions are enormous. However, our experience has taught us that it is extremely beneficial for you to try to find even a few minutes, though the longer the better, to have a conversation with yourself about what the specific death means to you before you speak about it with your child. As both Russ and Melanie discovered, every death or serious illness brings with it thoughts—both those we are aware of and those that lie in the recesses of our minds—of previous deaths that we have experienced. They may be hard to think about in a direct manner but, if not addressed, they will find other means of expression—perhaps as anger, uncontrollable crying, irritability, frustration, lack of focus, pessimism—that will complicate a conversation with your child.

TAKEAWAY
Asking yourself questions before talking with your child can help prepare you for the conversation.

Some of these questions may help you to work through the tumult of feelings brought on by a death:

WHO WAS THE PERSON WHO DIED?

o   What did the person mean to you?

o   How will their death impact you in your daily life?

WHAT REACTIONS ARE YOU HAVING TO THIS DEATH?

o What are some of the feelings you are experiencing around the death? Try to pinpoint them—maybe you feel sadness, anger, relief, disbelief, or numbness. Perhaps you are vulnerable or scared?

o Are you feeling survivor's guilt that you are alive when someone else has died?

o Are you judging yourself for your feelings?

o Did you expect to feel this way?

o Are you worried about loved ones?

WHAT OTHER EXPERIENCES HAVE YOU HAD WITH SEVERE ILLNESS OR DEATH?

o What was your first experience with death?

o What was your reaction then and to other illnesses or deaths?

o Are you responding in a similar way now?

o Have you ever really thought about those deaths since they occurred?

o Do you think you processed them thoroughly?

WHAT IS YOUR OWN CONCEPT OF DEATH?

o Does thinking about death in general make you afraid?

o If so, can you find a reason for that in your past?

o How does thinking about your own mortality feel?

o How did your own parents influence you around thinking about death?

o What do you believe happens after death?

o What prompts these feelings?

o How do your culture, religion, or spiritual beliefs impact your thoughts?

WHAT HELPS YOU TO COPE WITH STRESS?

o Do you prefer time alone or talking it out?

o Do you tend to delve into it in your mind or distract yourself?

o What self-care helps you? Music? Being active? Meditation? Prayer? Getting together with friends?

WHAT ARE YOUR THOUGHTS ABOUT TALKING TO YOUR CHILD?

o What are you worried about regarding your child's reaction?

o Are you comfortable being with your child when he is upset? Or do you rush in to fix the situation?

We explore another best practice, *Know your child*, in more detail in Chapter 7. It can be of use here as you think about how your child might react and how you can best help your child navigate those reactions.

The questions you ask yourself may cause emotional discomfort as they bring you face-to-face with the reality of death, but they will also help you to see the complex and interlaced network of thoughts and feelings that loss can create. Once brought to the surface, even in a rudimentary way, they can be acknowledged and given attention. It can be useful, if time and circumstances allow, to talk through some of these questions with a spouse, partner, or friend. Or perhaps with a therapist or religious advisor. You could write them down. In these ways, you gain some control over your reaction, some idea of what is most likely to set off an emotional response, and are less likely to be taken by surprise by your own behavior. If you know what you're feeling, you'll be able to weather the ins and outs of your child's response to the news with more equanimity. When you are caught up in unrecognized feelings within your own reactions to a loss, it is more difficult for you to give your attention to your child's reactions. This can make a challenging situation harder to experience for everyone. Once you have addressed your own thoughts and feelings, you will feel more prepared to focus on your child.

TAKEAWAY

Steadying yourself before talking with your child allows you to focus more on her and her needs.

Atul and Priya were thrilled to be expecting their second daughter in several months' time and were relieved that four-year-old Leena seemed to be excited, too. She already referred to her as "my baby" and knew the games she and her sister would play. One rainy Saturday, she pulled out the big box of old clothes from the back of the closet and chose her favorite outfits for her new sister. "Let's put them here. With mine," she insisted, opening her dresser drawer. Her parents smiled. "You'll be a great big sister," said her mom.

A week later, Priya woke up with tremendous cramps and back pain and immediately knew something was wrong. "She's not moving," she said to Atul, her hands on her stomach. Where before she had felt the baby's undulations, now there was nothing. Just stillness. A visit to her doctor confirmed the absence of a heartbeat, a miscarriage at twenty weeks. She would have to return for surgery in a few days. The doctor's words, delivered with kindness, made

Priya vomit. She and Atul wept in each other's arms before heading out to the parking lot and driving home.

"We have to tell Leena," said Atul sadly.

But when they arrived home, Priya was in some pain and went to bed for the rest of the day. Atul was able to tell Leena that her mother wasn't feeling well and, just before her bedtime, the little girl came to give a good-night kiss. "Good night, Mommy. Good night, my baby," she sang out as she left. When the door closed, Priya burst into tears.

The next day, Priya spent the morning in bed listening to calming music. She and Atul planned to tell Leena the bad news that afternoon. He would pick her up from preschool, bring her home for lunch, and then they would all sit down together and talk. Until then, they tried to distract themselves.

Later, Priya forced herself out of bed, took a deep breath, and joined her husband and daughter in the living room. "Mommy!" shouted Leena. "Are you better?" She leaped off the couch and ran toward her mother. "Your baby sister isn't living anymore!" Priya blurted, then stopped, horrified. It wasn't what they had planned at all. Leena immediately started to bawl. Priya just stared, taking in her small daughter's shocked face, her wail of misery, but she did nothing to comfort her. She couldn't. She felt ice-cold, unable to talk or move. If she opened her mouth, she thought she might scream. Atul, tearful himself, gently took Leena's hand and led her back to the couch, where he cradled her, telling her that Mommy was very, very upset about the baby. Priya turned away and went to her bedroom, where she sat on the end of the bed, trying to fathom what had happened.

The next day Priya came to see Elena and told her story, wanting to know the best way forward with Leena, with Atul, and with her own grieving. As she listened, Elena asked about Priya's previous experiences with death and learned that her parents had communicated with her openly and honestly from the time she was small. Her grandparents had died when she was in her teens and she seemed to have processed their deaths. Her mother had died just before Leena was born and her father was still alive and in good health. She didn't seem to have excessive fear around death and her instinct had been to tell the truth to Leena. However, as Priya talked, it became clear that she had not checked in with herself fully about this recent death, that of her unborn child. She had not allowed herself to think how much of a loss it was to her. It had taken her and Atul several years to conceive and the stress had weighed on their marriage.

In speaking with Elena, Priya realized that she was scared that now she would not have another baby, that she and Atul might grow distant again, that Leena would be damaged by the death of the baby she had loved so much. She hadn't processed any of this before speaking to her daughter, and her terror at losing everything she held dear had made her rush the news out. Then, in her horror over her words, she had pushed all her feelings inside, trying to contain them lest she say something else that might be hurtful. Now, in Elena's office, she cried, all her emotions returning in a rush. Together they came up with a plan for Priya to talk to Atul, who would be grieving, too, and for the two of them to sit down with Leena.

The following morning, Priya made hot chocolate and invited Leena to join her at the kitchen table. She apologized for not hugging her when she was crying and asked if it would be okay to do so now.

"Hugs are back?" Leena asked.

Priya nodded and her daughter scrambled into her lap. Later, with Elena's help, Priya would talk with Atul about their relationship, and together they would have ongoing conversations with Leena about the death of the baby. But for right now, this hug was the place to start.

Parents play a critical role in their children's emotional development, and this is especially true in situations where feelings are heightened. The process of parenting often includes helping children to manage their emotions and can affect a parent's own emotional state. In the face of a child's distress, parents can find it challenging to control their own feelings and this, in turn, affects their child. On a regular day, you may be called on to read your child's emotions, help her identify them, validate her experience, and engage in problem-solving, all while handling the many feelings that may arise for you in the process. It is a formidable task. If you are also coping with the death of someone you love, it is especially demanding. In suggesting that you first assess your own response to a death, we hope to make the process of talking to your child easier. While it may seem overwhelming at first, we know that many parents find it can be relieving. When you fit your own oxygen mask first, this best practice gives you permission to pause and check in with yourself. A period of self-reflection enables you to harness inner resources to regulate your own emotions, and then to move quickly and effectively to tend to your child. By taking the time to help yourself, you can respond with empathy to your child's needs, wrapping her in kindness in a way that supports and strengthens her.

Children look to their parents for guidance on how to act and will take note of their emotions as well as their words. When Russ sat down with his children again to talk with them about his father's failing health and his sadness about his mother's death, he learned how they had felt about seeing him break down uncontrollably in front of them.

"It was scary, Daddy," said Mia. "I didn't like that."

"No cry," added Jaden, covering his ears.

"I wish I had been here to help you all," said Michelle. "I'm here now." She squeezed Russ's hand.

"I'm sorry," said Russ. "My feelings were so strong that I wasn't able to handle them. I wasn't ready. But now, I've had a chance to breathe deeply and to think things through. I still have feelings of sadness—and that's okay—but I know now that I was thinking about my mom, who you didn't get to meet. Talking about her and remembering her is helping a lot."

That Sunday, the whole family went to visit Gramps at his home. He introduced them to Maria, a home aide who visited him to help with daily tasks. She made pancakes just the way he and the children loved them.

"You remember how Mom stacked the pancakes high?" said Russ. "They seemed like mountains when I was a kid."

His father looked at him for a second, then nodded. "She was a good cook, your mom was. I miss her."

After breakfast, Russ talked with his father about his childhood and about his mother, and Gramps brought out photographs for Mia, Jaden, and Michelle to see. Then, the children listened for the first time to stories about the grandmother they had never met.

TAKEAWAY

Painful though it may seem, processing your own feelings about an illness or death will help you. It will aid in resolving grief from the past.

Looking deeply within may seem painful, especially if you are already stressed about a recent death, but this kind of reflection can help to ground you in the moment, and over time it may bring relief and a feeling of hope as you come to terms with prior losses and process unresolved emotions. In many ways, this removal of emotional splinters can lead to a well-earned sense of mastery. Russ was finally able to confront his feelings about his mother's death and bring her back into his life and share her with his family. Melanie told her children tales about Smudge and Birdie, further empathizing with them over the loss of their beloved Riley and allowing herself to enjoy the memories of her own childhood pets. Maybe one day when they were older she would tell them about the way her parents dealt with Smudge's death, but not now. That was not their burden to carry. Priya would incorporate the loss of her unborn child into her personal story and into her conversations with her husband and daughter. She would realize that Atul was deeply upset, too, and that they both needed to take care of each other. This awareness would lead to a more cohesive grieving process and, in a few months' time, they would plant a tree together in memory, joined together by their shared and openly expressed sorrow.

When parents take the courageous step to turn away from avoidance and to reflect on past and present experiences with death, it readies them to talk with their children about death. With their emotions more balanced, they can focus on their child.

Chapter 4

Seizing the Opportunity to Talk About Death

Michael was walking with his friends Polly and Walt and their young family in the woods near his home, enjoying a break from the usual routine. The children had all rushed a little way ahead, crunching through leaves, and whooping their delight. Sometimes one of them would stop and pick up a woodland treasure—a branch, mossy rock, or prickly horse chestnut—and examine the item before dropping it and dashing through the trees again. Polly, a doctor, was retelling a story one of her nurses had told earlier in the week when suddenly all three children came to a halt. They gathered around the eldest, Jamie, peering at something cupped in his hands. As the grown-ups grew closer, Michael observed a small brown frog stretched out in Jamie's palm, its soft belly facing up.

"It's dead," said Evie, her small face solemn.

"It died of a heart attack," added Jamie.

"We should bury it," said Ben, aged four, the youngest of the siblings.

Together, the children cleared a small patch at the base of a towering oak and dug a hole. Jamie laid the frog in the dirt and Evie and Ben covered it with a blanket of leaves. Next, they stood side by side, heads lowered, silent, until Jamie said, "Rest in peace, Froggy," and his siblings echoed him. They stayed there for another minute, the wind rustling in the branches overhead, then Evie shouted, "Come on!" Off they ran, leaping over tree roots, along the path.

Later as Michael followed his friends back toward the car, he couldn't get the incident out of his mind. The children had incorporated the frog's death into their afternoon's fun, giving it time and attention before returning to their play. They had not seemed alarmed or upset by the subject but accepted it for what it was, part of the grand scheme of things within the natural world. They spoke openly about the frog's death, grasped something about burial and the language around such rituals. Clearly they were aware of the concept of death, but Michael wondered how much they understood about how it applied to them or their loved ones. Did they know that their parents would die one day? That they themselves would die? And if they did know, at least in an abstract way, was it something they thought about?

When Michael asked his friends if they had spoken with their children about death, they shook their heads.

"We haven't avoided it but we haven't embraced it, either," said Polly. "They seem to just know. They haven't experienced any personal deaths—we've been lucky. And they haven't asked us any awkward questions so far."

"Thank goodness," said Walt. "Whatever would we say?"

We believe that parents should try to have a conversation about illness and death whenever their child shows curiosity rather than waiting for a loss to happen. For some children, this could be as young as the age of three, but it will be different for each child. The idea is to educate your child and let him know that death is a subject that can be talked about, just like any other. Children already have inklings about death and are curious about it as part of their expanding knowledge of the world around them, and they do not approach it as something to be automatically feared. We understand that talking about the concept of death before a personal loss occurs is not always possible and that you may have come to this book for help with specific loss—and we offer you our support and guidance at this difficult time in our other chapters.

Here we provide practical outlines for parents who have decided they would like to talk to their young child about the serious subject of death. The reasons could be many. Perhaps a coworker suffered a death in his family recently, had to break the news to his children, and this got you thinking. Maybe a school shooting was covered in the news and while your child is very young still, you want to be able to frame the narrative yourself. Or possibly your child has been asking questions after seeing a movie and you don't want to tiptoe around the subject anymore. We know it is likely that you don't want to have this conversation, but if you have made the brave choice to do so, we would like to support your decision and to help you feel comfortable as you take the steps to talk to your child. We believe you will be very glad you did.

Once you have made the decision to talk about death, we recommend that you follow the best practice discussed in Chapter 3— *Know your own thoughts and feelings*—before speaking with your child. This will help you to understand your own vulnerabilities, and to balance yourself so that you are able to steady your emotions as much as possible. Your thoughts and responses will prepare you for questions that your child may have. We encourage you to return to Chapter 3 to refresh your memory, and have compiled a list of additional questions here that you might find especially useful now.

QUESTIONS ABOUT YOU

- How did you learn about death as a young child?

- Do you remember how you felt about it?

- How do you think your first experiences with death have shaped you?

- How did you process them?

- What helped you with your grieving process?

QUESTIONS ABOUT YOUR CHILD

- What experiences has your child had about death, in life, nature, books, TV, video games, and movies?

- Has your child asked you about death in the past?

- How does your child usually express emotions?

o   Does your child like affection and touch when you are talking? Does he like to color or play with toys when you talk about potentially big things?

o   Does your child surprise you with emotions sometimes? How have you responded in the past to that?

Once you feel clearheaded and ready to move forward, we find that the best approach is to look for a conversation opener. In most cases, we recommend an informal chat embedded in a typical daily conversation, rather than a formal sit-down with your child in which you discuss death. Allow your words to arise from something else, just as other conversations do with your child, on topics large and small. If Michael's friends, Polly and Walt, were looking for an opening to start a conversation with their children, then the discovery of the dead frog might have paved the way.

TAKEAWAY

Conversations with your child about what death is are best begun by taking cues from your child's world/ environment.

Now that you have made the courageous decision to speak with your child, you will probably notice that your ears are finely attuned to possible introductions. It could be a moment as simple as seeing a bouquet of wilting daffodils on the kitchen counter and saying, "I'm so sad that my birthday flowers have died." Or perhaps your child notices a fly on the windowsill, upside down and still, and says, "Why isn't the fly moving?" Questions such as these occur very often with young children. Many parents dodge them and come up with an answer that moves the subject along. "Because that's what flowers do. But we can bring in some more from the yard, would you like to?" or "Oh, that silly fly. It looks like it's taking a nap." These answers might satisfy your child in the moment, but their brains will continue to cogitate around the questions they asked. Many children, even very young ones, may pick up on your hesitation or awkwardness as you answer (or avoid the question), especially if it happens often, and will begin to sense that this is not an easy topic for you. Once you have resolved to find an opportunity to talk with your child about death, you'll find that these types of situations are natural ways to begin a discussion.

So how might a conversation go once you've found what feels like an opportune moment? We have suggestions on both the content of your words—the information you convey—and also your delivery— the way in which you package the content. First, we'll address the content. In Chapter 2 we mentioned four important elements that you would want to communicate to your child for them to have a full understanding of death:

Universality

Put simply, this means that all living things—plants, animals, people—must eventually die. A forest of trees will glimmer with new leaves and blossom in the spring, then cycle through the seasons until branches are bare, and foliage and flowers long dead. A caterpillar turns into a butterfly that perishes when days grow cold. The cycle of life can be helpful as an explanation that every living thing comes to be, lives, and then dies. As children take in this information, some believe there are exclusions for themselves and the people they love, that they can magically avoid death, or keep it at bay through luck or cunning. It will be important that you help your child to understand that everyone dies—though not necessarily in your first conversation. As you'll see later in the chapter, we have ways to help you give your child this information.

Irreversibility

This means that death is permanent. It is essential that children understand that once the physical body has died, it cannot be made alive again. Some children see death as reversible, as something fleeting such as sleep or a trip, and believe that it is possible to wake up or return from it. One of Elena's young patients was told that his grandma had died and reacted to the news with tears. He was very close to her and they spent a lot of time together, as they lived in the same house. Later, at dinner, he asked, "When will Grandma be here?" The idea of permanence can be hard to grasp. Sometimes children think that medical intervention can reverse a death, something as simple as taking a pill, or that a dead person can be revived if they eat or drink something to give them strength. Others believe in magical spells or wishful thinking. While it may be easy to see where such thoughts come from, as we live in a world in which flattened, supposedly dead characters spring back to life in cartoons and video games, and fairy-tale princesses often elude death, the important point is to help your child comprehend that death is forever. When you state that the physical body dies and cannot return to life, it leaves room to incorporate cultural and religious beliefs about life after death if those have meaning for you. We will address this later in the chapter.

Finality

Sometimes referred to as "non-functionality," this element means that once a living thing dies, all life-defining capabilities cease. In other words, dead beings cannot do the things that the living do. The dead fly on the windowsill will no longer soar into the air; the small brown frog, buried under moss, cannot leap or swim; a deceased human will not eat or see or think. Again, an emphasis on the physical body allows you to discuss the idea of what a spirit may be able to do if your belief system includes a concept of an afterlife.

Causality

This refers to the concept that death occurs for many different reasons, though ultimately the cause of death is the failure of internal body organs. Young children may believe that unrealistic reasons—such as their unkind thoughts or behavior—can bring about death (which can lead to feelings of shame and guilt). Not all children may have the heart attack diagnosis at their fingertips, as Walt and Polly's son did, and for many children it is difficult to grasp the concept that a person dies because her body fails to function. As the parent, you can be extremely helpful in parsing this information.

We are not suggesting that you have a detailed conversation with your young child about these four fundamentals of death. Instead, we offer them so you can be aware of what your child may grapple with as she tries to understand the concept. We recommend that you start small, keep things simple, and don't go into too many details. Notice your child's reaction and take your lead from her, aiming to keep a balance between providing enough information and not over-whelming her. You should expect to have a series of conversations over time. Some will be do-overs and some may repeat the same information. Be patient with your child and with yourself—this is a process and perfection is not the goal.

In the next few chapters, we provide best practices to help you navigate conversations with your child about a specific loss that has impacted your family. Some of these best practices apply when you are speaking to your child about the concept of death, and we recommend that you look at Chapters 6 through 8 before you embark on a conversation.

The day after his walk in the woods with his friends, Michael received a phone call from Walt.

"I thought you might like to know," he said, "this morning, Ben, our youngest, asked if we could go to the woods again. He said he wanted to see if the frog had woken up from its nap."

It turned out that even though Ben had participated in the frog's funeral and had been the one to suggest burying it, he was not aware of the permanence of death. Walt was surprised.

If Walt were to use the frog as an opening, his conversation might go something like this:

Walt: Ben, have you been thinking that the frog is sleeping?

Ben: Yes.

Walt: When we say something is dead, it can't be sleeping. Being dead is very different from sleeping. When the frog died, its body stopped working and cannot ever work again.

Ben: Because its heart attacked him? Like Jamie said?

Walt: Well, we don't know for sure why it died. But we do know it can't be alive ever again.

Ben: It can't wake up?

Walt: No. When living creatures sleep, their bodies are resting but they are still doing things they do as part of being alive, like breathing, moving maybe, dreaming.

Ben: Snoring.

Walt: Yes. Like snoring. But the frog is dead and cannot breathe or move or do any of those things like swimming or leaping that it did when it was alive.

Ben: I am sad.

Walt (*giving Ben a hug*): Yes, it is sad. We can be sad together. It might help you to know that you paid attention to the frog and found a safe place for its body to be.

Walt (*after a short silence*): Do you want to talk about it some more?

Ben: No. I'm hungry now.

Walt: Okay, we can talk about it another time if you like. Let's go and make grilled cheese sandwiches for lunch.

In this very simple and open conversation, Walt introduces his young son to the elements of irreversibility (the frog cannot be alive again), finality (the frog can no longer do living frog things), and causality (the frog died for a reason, though they are unsure what). Walt did not move on to discussing universality—that all living things must eventually die—as Ben was ready to finish their chat.

A conversation may move forward simply, keeping a narrow focus, or it might cover more ground, extending to incorporate other scenarios. Sometimes a child will transfer her new knowledge to herself—"Will I die?"—or to you or other loved ones—"Will you die? Will Grandma Edith die?" You should have a simple response for such questions if they arise (and we provide an example below), but if your child doesn't ask, we suggest that you not offer ideas about other people. Instead, we advise that you stay with where your child is in processing what death means, knowing that she will have other queries at another time and you can be ready for them then. It is always wise to ask, "Do you have any questions?" before ending a conversation, so that your child might bring forth a question that is swirling in her mind but she was too timid to ask. If she doesn't have anything else on her mind at that time, we recommend saying that she can ask you about it again anytime she wants, just as Walt did with Ben, and that you might bring it up, too, if ideas occur to you.

Caroline and Dara came to see Elena because their five-year-old daughter, Madison, had been asking them a lot of questions about death. Madison had watched the movie *Moana* and the scene of

Moana's grandmother on her deathbed had made her cry. Since then she had become clingier and wanted the light on in her room as she was falling asleep.

"Madison called her grandma—my mom—to ask her if she would die, too," said Dara. "I felt so bad. My mom got mad at me about it."

Madison's grandma ignored her question, and when she asked her parents whether her grandma would die, they said no. Dara and Caroline felt uneasy about their lie and asked Elena for help in revisiting the conversation. This is how it went.

Caroline: Do you remember when you asked us if your grandma was going to die and we said no?

Madison: Yes.

Dara: Well, that isn't true. Grandma is healthy now and she takes medicines to keep her well and sees the doctor, so we don't expect her to die soon, but one day, when you are much older, she will die.

Madison: Oh, I don't want that to happen to Grandma.

Caroline: I know, honey. We don't want that to happen, either. We will be very sad.

Madison: And you? Will you die?

Dara: Well, I take very good care of my body and I do all the things doctors tell me to do to stay as healthy as possible and to live as long as I can. But one day, maybe when I am much older and you are all grown up, it will happen and you will be prepared.

Caroline: And so do I. I plan to live as long as possible.

Madison: In the movie, Moana's grandma comes back to her as a spirit and is nice to her. Maybe that will happen with Grandma.

Caroline: Would you like that?

Madison: Yes. Can I call Grandma now?

Dara: Yes, of course. Do you have any more questions now?

Madison: No.

Caroline: Okay, well if you think of any, you know you can ask us anytime.

Children are very literal in their comprehension of big ideas, and your child's questions may be very direct. Madison touched on a topic that many children are curious about—"What happens after death?"—but she seemed content with not asking anything more about it. Dara and Caroline will be prepared to answer when their daughter is ready to broach the subject. When your child asks you about the afterlife or what happens after death, we recommend that you have some version of an answer in mind, but we suggest that you ask your child first what *he* thinks in response to this question.

"What happens after death?" can be met with "What do *you* think happens?"

It's interesting to note that as children grow older, they are able to engage with the idea that someone can be dead and so cannot function as a living being anymore and yet they can still see, speak, think, and send love in spirit form. When children are asked what they think happens after death, they tend to describe the idea that a loved one has moved to some other place in some other form, such as a spirit or an angel. This is especially, but not only, true if a family's faith reinforces that perspective.

It is your choice as a parent to share your spiritual beliefs with your child, and we understand that you might choose to teach him your held belief system while helping him to grasp the concept of death. We recommend, though, that you try not to judge any ideas that your child may have about what happens after death, even if they do not reflect your own views. His ideas are still evolving and his understanding is still developing, so if he believes that people go to live in the clouds after they die while you are an atheist, we would encourage you to listen and help him elaborate his thoughts. As he matures, you and he will be able to have many discussions on the subject, but for now it is important to convey that you hear his ideas and be as open as you can to letting his beliefs exist without imposing your own. In this way, you model for your child the gift of listening and considering what someone else has to say even if you disagree. These ideas about death and afterlife serve as ballasts against fears sometimes, and your child may be expressing that he needs that idea right now. As you help your child to understand his world, with a flow of thoughts and ideas, you create an empathic connection with him.

Just as Madison started to think about the death of those close to her after seeing *Moana*, for many young children, books and movies may be their first introduction to the idea of loss. Disney and Pixar movies, rife with deaths of multiple characters, both human and animal, can be excellent avenues for adults to engage children in conversations about death and dying. These conversations can provide means for children to develop comfort and ease instead of shock around the subject of death. Fairy tales, including those made into Disney movies, have been around for hundreds of years to help explain the mysteries of the world to children and adults alike and can also jump-start conversations. "Hansel and Gretel" tells the tale of two children sent into the woods to die and ends with the children pushing the evil witch into her own oven. The wolf in "The Three Little Pigs" meets a similarly gruesome fate in a pot of boiling water, while the villainous queen demands Snow White's heart as proof of her death. And there are plenty of other examples you might choose to discuss with your child. There are many children's books that specifically address the subject of loss and can be a very intentional way of talking to a child about it. We provide a list of helpful books in our Resources section.

We would advise that you take the time to consider your child's potential reaction to any books and movies before you use them as a way to open a conversation about death. And if during watching or reading, your child shows discomfort or asks to stop, then be respectful of his wish. It can be especially tempting to say, "Don't worry, you'll be fine," when the alternative is bothering other moviegoers in a crowded theater. But follow your child's cues. You can talk with your child afterward about what was uncomfortable to him and see if you can provide another opportunity—with planning beforehand—to have him approach the experience another day.

As you start to attune yourself to your child's curiosity around life and death, and to find conversation starters in the world around you, you may find your relationship deepening. Your child will see that he can talk to you about anything and everything, big and small. It's the start of something wonderful. We know families that have started a weekly check-in with their young children, a family circle time when everyone can voice whatever's on their mind or in their hearts. It's an excellent idea to set up this communication bridge when children are young. We hope that you'll find that embracing difficult conversations with your child will bring rich rewards for you both.

TAKEAWAY

Being responsive to your child wanting to understand death will deepen the connection between you.

Chapter 5

The Who, When, Where, What, and How to Tell

❋ Sharing Difficult News ❋ Gathering as a Family ❋

❋ Finding a Time and Place ❋ Language to Use About Death ❋

❋ Dialogue for Breaking the News ❋ Children's Common Questions ❋

❋ An Ongoing Conversation ❋ Expressing Emotion During Telling ❋

❋ Non-Verbal Communication ❋ Promoting Trust Through Truth ❋

One Memorial Day, over ten years ago, Michael received a phone call. On answering, he heard a voice blurt out, "Michael, David's dead." Every Memorial Day since then, the phone call has replayed in his head and he feels that same sense of shock. He returns to the moment when he learned about the sudden death of a beloved friend. No one likes to give or receive the news of the death or serious illness of a loved one, and it is not easy to be part of such a conversation. However, there are some ways of imparting information that can ease the process for both the bearer and recipient of bad news.

Almost daily in our work as therapists and in school communities, we are asked, "But what should I say?" or "How can we possibly tell the kids?" We know that when parents don't know how to answer these questions, or are not confident in their abilities to address them, they often find themselves struggling to communicate effectively. In this chapter, we provide you with tools, language, and structure to have that most difficult of conversations: telling a child about the death or serious illness of someone they love. We will walk you through the process and help you to find the strength and words you need.

While there is certainly a moment when parents choose the words to tell their child about a painful change in their life, those sentences will be the beginning, not the end, of a conversation. In our experience, "breaking the news" is a process in evolution, as your child will be learning and relearning about a loss over and over again as he matures. A child may be given a four-year-old version of a grandparent's death but will also need a six-year-old version, a ten-year-old version, and a thirteen-year-old version to be able to reprocess his emotions. Each of these conversations will be an ongoing "breaking the news," and you'll find over time that your mutual understanding grows within these open, caring conversations. This can be a comfort for you, as you will have many chances

to give your child the support
and skills he needs to get
through a loss and to read-
dress ways in which you may
wish you had handled something differently.

That being said, we have
recommendations for the initial sharing of news, a frame-
work made up of best practices that will ease you through that first
conversation with your child and help you find the language to tell
him about a loss.

First, we encourage you to take the time to follow the best practice *Know your own thoughts and feelings.* As we discussed in Chapter
3, this practice enables you to explore the impact the death of your
loved one is having on you, to acknowledge your emotions, and to
try to find a sense of equilibrium. It can be helpful to speak with a
partner or friend, therapist or religious advisor, or to express your
feelings in writing as a way to begin to understand and regulate your
emotions. We are not suggesting that you hide your feelings from
your child. Instead, we know that processing them will help you feel
less disoriented and more measured. In doing so, when you speak
with your child your focus can be on him, not on you.

Who

Once you feel ready to tell your child—and we recommend not leaving it too long—it's best to have two adults involved, if possible, to
break the news. In this way, you can support each other, and take
turns in speaking, if necessary, if one feels overwhelmed. If there are
two connected parents in your child's life, then you should give the
news together as a family, if feasible.

TAKEAWAY

Telling your child about a
death is really a process of
many conversations rather
than a single one breaking
the news.

TAKEAWAY
Break the news of a death
with all members of the
family together when
possible.

If not, the child's primary caregiver and another trusted adult are the ones who should share the information. In having this conversation, your aim is to make your child feel secure with the truth. Your love for your child as well as your knowledge of your child's emotional reactions and coping mechanisms mean you are best equipped for this role.

If a parent—or parental figure—is the loved one who has died, then an additional adult is especially important to buoy you or to take over the primary role of telling your child. This support is practical and also sends the child a message that there are other loving adults in her life who will continue to look after her and take care of her.

There are other instances, too, when telling as a family is not possible. You may be too devastated and consumed by your own grief or too traumatized to speak or even to be present. In such a situation, it is still important for your child to be told so that she knows what is happening. We encourage you to designate someone else (a partner, relative, or caregiver) to share the news. One of Michael's patients was in a car accident in which he was injured and his father—his child's grandfather—died. The patient's wife, with the support of her sister, gave their children the sad news about Grandpa and explained that Dad was recovering in the hospital. In all cases in which one or both parents cannot be present when news about an illness or loss is shared, we recommend that children are given a calm explanation as to why. This would include a reference to a future time when the parent(s) will be available to talk to their child.

We recommend that siblings should be told at the same time, if at all possible, even children whom you might believe are too young to understand the news you are sharing. One of Elena's patients, a single parent, learned about the death of her mother late one night. The next morning she told her nine-year-old son about Gran, talking with him and giving him hugs, before heading downstairs. She planned to tell her six-year-old daughter as soon as she woke up—she had looked so peaceful sleeping still. In the meantime, the mom was inundated with calls from relatives wishing her well. As she finished up a conversation, she heard sobbing from upstairs, and rushed to her daughter's bedroom. There she found her, wailing under her bed, while her big brother stood by looking distressed. It turned out that he had told his sister, "You'll never see Gran again! She's dead!" The young girl had been especially close to Gran and the way she heard the news about her death—without an introduction to prepare her and without her mother around—devastated her. It took her mom a while to help her become a little calmer. In this case, the abrupt delivery of the news by her brother, combined with his understandable inability to handle her explosive reaction, worsened her already significant pain.

Whenever possible, it is helpful for you to be able to control the information your child receives, and it is easier to do so if everyone hears the initial news at the same time and in the same way. If there is a large age difference between children, such as a five-year-old and a thirteen-year-old, we recommend an initial breaking of the news with everyone present in which you would speak to the youngest level. Then, if the older child has specific questions that go beyond what a younger child needs to hear, we recommend responding, "Why don't we talk together in a little while so we can answer your questions." During that subsequent conversation, we would add, "If you feel like talking with your brother, please bear in mind that he is much younger than you. Think about how he might respond to anything you say and if you do talk to him, let me know just so I'm aware." This is preferable to banning older siblings from discussing an illness or death with younger siblings, and it is a way to help them navigate conversations between siblings that may come up. It would also be important to assure your older child that you will fill in more details for the younger child as he matures. With the initial breaking of the news, the message to convey is that the information affects everyone and that it is a time for the whole family to come together to share the experience.

When

It is best to choose a time—if you have the luxury of choice—when the whole family can be together for a while, both while giving the news and after it has been delivered. In this way, you can stay with your child as he considers and processes the information, and be ready for questions, or to help with emotional responses.

> **TAKEAWAY**
>
> Try to find a time to tell your child about a death when you can be with her for a while—and as far from bedtime as possible.

Early in the weekend is a good idea if that fits in with everyone's work and school commitments and is soon after the person has died. It provides an extended period of togetherness as a family, time for you to notice how your child is faring, a feeling of continuity for questions that may come up, and a general sense of getting through something in one another's company. But that may not be ideal for every family. Another option would be on a weekday after everyone is home from school, work, and daytime responsibilities, but as far away from bedtime as possible. It is better not to wait too long after the death has occurred to break the news, minimizing the chance that your child hears it from someone else, such as an older sibling. That would take away your ability to determine the narrative and to present the information with your child's best interests in mind.

Martin, one of Michael's patients, delayed telling his young son about the death of the boy's aunt. He was just too devastated to do so. Instead the little boy found out by overhearing a phone conversation. The boy's subsequent sadness and confusion led to night terrors and severe separation anxiety that compounded Martin's grief. "I should have just told him," he said to Michael. "I shouldn't have waited."

Telling children about death is difficult and "just telling" is easier said than done, but our years of experience have shown us that giving children news of a death in a timely manner is almost always the best option.

While you might deliver the news of a death by making a phone call, many teens and pre-teens tend to prefer contact by text or social media. Information can travel at lightning speed and be aware that, even without his own phone, your child might have knowledge or inklings of a death within hours of it happening.

For some parents, the only option for sharing the news may be in the morning before school. If your child learns that someone very close to him has died, we feel that it would be wise to have him stay home from school after hearing the news to provide him with the comfort of togetherness. While we usually speak to the importance of keeping children's routines in place as much as possible after a death, in this instance, we would err on the side of closeness rather than independence. In later chapters, we'll go into more details about the role of routine and school after a death.

Even with the best intentions and most detailed plans, you may not always be in control of exactly when to break bad news to your child. In such a situation, we recommend you follow your child's cues. For example, Elena's friend learned that his father-in-law had just died after several days in the hospital. The plan was to wait for his wife to come home so they could tell their young son about the death together. However, before she returned, the child asked, "Did Grandpa die?" It was a startling question. Elena's friend thought about saying nothing or stating that he didn't know, but after a moment's pause, he said, "Yes, I just found out. I feel very sad about it." He then sat with his son to talk with him about the upsetting news, letting him know they could continue the conversation when his mom came home.

Where

When you have decided on the right time for your family, gather everyone together in one place. Around the kitchen table or in the living room, whatever feels right for you, a place where everyone will feel at home and at ease. It is preferable to stay away from your child's room, or somewhere they specifically use as a calming place, so that these locations do not become associated with news of the death. Even so, bear in mind that the conversation may leave indelible imprints no matter where you choose, as often happens with pivotal events. We also recommend not telling your child while she is in the car. Many parents do have important conversations with their children while driving them places, as it is often uninterrupted time with a captive audience and little eye contact. But this particular conversation needs your physical presence, your ability to be attuned to your child's reactions, in addition to your voice giving her information.

> **TAKEAWAY**
> Have the conversation in a comfortable place where you can face each other with all screens turned off—and not in your child's bedroom.

A quiet and private setting is the best choice, with all screens—televisions, computers, phones, etc.—turned off, so that everyone can be entirely directed toward the conversation and there is little chance of interruption. Sometimes parents think it may be best to have the television on in the background to add a sense of normalcy, or to be busy with a task like folding laundry so the conversation seems less formal. We recommend instead that the focus remain on the words that are about to be said and on your child. The conversation need not be intense, but it is important and everyone should be able to give it their full attention. Try to sit face-to-face and in a setting where you can readily have body contact, such as hugs and holding hands. As children are hearing the news and processing it, they will find this nearness comforting. It can be helpful to have a familiar activity in mind for after everyone has sat together with the news, perhaps coloring books or jigsaw puzzles, so it is a good idea to have those on hand.

What

When everyone is together in one place, has settled down, and is listening, it is best to begin.

For the breaking of the news, start simply. "We have some unhappy news to tell you. We just found out that Uncle Danny died. It's very sad, and we're all going to spend some time together." Take a breath before you begin and again between each part, as it can help you to feel more centered.

TAKEAWAY

In general, for breaking the news, you will make a brief statement that there is some sad news to share now, then state what has happened, and conclude with a sentence that you will all spend some time together.

Be thoughtful about the language you use to explain a death and remember that children are very concrete in their understanding. We recommend using the word "died." Its direct simplicity leaves no room for misinterpretation. Often parents want to protect their child and so soften the blow by using words that seem less harsh. They may also have been raised with vague words to signify that someone has died, such as "She passed away," "She slipped away," "He is resting in peace," "He took his last breath," or "He's in a better place now." These euphemisms can be confusing for young children, and it is likely that a child who is told that her uncle Danny has slipped away will have no idea that he has died. Other examples of phrases best avoided include: "We lost him," "She went away," or "He is gone." With these a child may think there's the chance that her uncle might be found, or her grandma may return, or that she could visit her soccer coach wherever he has gone. There's also the possibility that a child may worry that anytime someone gets lost or goes away (to the store, on a trip), it means that person has died and will never return.

It can be helpful in later conversations with your child to explain that other adults and children may use different expressions to describe death, some more veiled than others, and to share them with her. In this way, you would hope to lessen any confusion that might arise when she is exposed to other people's language.

After the initial breaking of the news, and before thinking about adding any details, it is a good idea to pause and let your child take in your statement. This pause allows children to find their reaction and should be free of your expectations. Depending on their age, their experience with death, and their feelings for the person who died, their understanding of—and their response to—your first words will vary. They may have questions or say nothing at all. They may burst into tears or just stare at you, or may react in a way that is somewhere in between. Every response is valid. We elaborate on specific reactions and how to handle them in Chapter 7. If your child has questions, respond to just as much as he is asking but do not offer more than that. If he wants more details after that, he will ask for more in a follow-up question then or later. Your child will need time to take in the information, so it's best to allow for pauses, even silence, and to leave space for questions as they emerge, even though that may feel awkward. Many parents rush to fill a silence with words but we advise against it. Sit with your child and take your cues from him, from what he needs from you now, rather than what you think he may need.

One of Elena's patients, Sue, had to break the news to her twin daughters after the sudden death of Becca, a close family friend. Sue received the news herself while at work and immediately went home, where her husband, Yves, joined her. Together they processed the shocking news. Several hours later, Yves picked up their seven-year-olds from school and he and Sue gathered everyone in the living room. We'll use their conversation as an example of how to break the news.

Sue: We have some sad news to share with you both. Our friend Becca died today.

(Both parents pause, letting the news sink in.)

Sue: Do you have any questions?

Emma: I can't . . . I love Becca.

Holly (crying): No.

Yves: It's a lot to take in. Let's just be together for a while.

(The family sits quietly for a few minutes.)

Sue: Is there anything you'd like to know?

Emma: How did she die?

Yves: She was hit by a car while crossing the street. Her body stopped working right away.

(Emma cries and her mother hugs her.)

Holly: I don't like that.

Yves: I know, sweetie. It is very upsetting.

(The family sits together, supporting one another, the girls crying softly.)

Sue: Do you have any more questions, girls?

Emma and Holly: No.

Yves: If you do, you can ask us anytime. And we'll check in with you both on how you're doing.

(They all stay together until it is time to prepare dinner.)

This is the basic structure for breaking the news. It wraps the children in simple honesty and togetherness to help them feel heard and included in the moment of receiving the news and into the future as they process the details further.

If the death or illness is that of a parent, or a parent figure, or someone especially close to the child and his life will likely change drastically, we recommend additional language. He will need to be reassured that his remaining parent or parent figure will continue to be there for him and his world will still have familiar structure.

These words, or a version of them, would be beneficial:

"I'm here to help you and we will go through this together. And there are many other people—Grandma Flo, Uncle Marvin, my friend Allie, Coach Evers—who are eager to spend time with you and help out. I'll also talk to your teachers and they will be there for you in school."

When a parent gives her child this information, she encourages him to see that life continues even when we are sad, that even very different feelings can co-exist. She may also feel reassured herself that she has her own community of support to help her and her child navigate this loss.

We provide additional advice to assist you in coping with a death in the immediate family in Chapter 13.

Common Questions

When Sue and Yves told their children about Becca's sudden death, Emma asked a question many children might have after learning such news. She wanted to know how their friend had died. Other common questions children may ask after you break the news are:

"Are you going to die, too?" "Where do people go when they die?" "Will we see him again?"

We have answered some of these questions in previous chapters and will return to them again, as they are questions that may preoccupy your child as he grapples with the idea—and reality—of death. His thoughts will likely change as he grows. We believe it is important for you to have an idea of how to answer such questions when the subject of death comes up or when specific deaths enter your life. It is best to answer exactly what your child asks and not more, as children tend to be concrete, especially when emotionally challenged. They can become overwhelmed, and it is more helpful to give answers that reveal too little with a stance that encourages more questions over time. Sometimes we adults use too many words in an attempt to feel helpful—and because we are anxious. This is one of those moments when less is more, at least initially.

How Did He Die?

Difficult as it may be, it is a good idea to have an answer to this question ready, and our recommendation is to keep it simple. For example, "She died of a disease called cancer." "His heart stopped working." "He was very old and his lungs didn't work anymore."

Are You Going to Die?

When your child asks some version of, "Are you going to die, too?" we suggest an answer such as "I plan to live a very, very, very long time. I go to the doctor for checkups just like you do, and we try to keep ourselves as healthy as we can."

Such an answer may not always alleviate a child's worries if, for example, the person died in an accident, as Becca did when crossing the street. In that case, we recommend saying, "What happened to Becca is very, very rare. Millions of people cross the street every day without getting hit by a car."

What Happens After You Die?

This answer is different for every family and is informed by culture, faith, and religion. It's important for parents to remember to keep things simple. Breaking the news is not a time for a philosophical discussion (though one may ensue over the years) but a moment to reassure your child. You might say, "We believe that after a person dies, they get another life as a different kind of being, such as an animal." Or, "We believe that Cousin Jacob has gone to heaven." Or, "We believe that though Grandma Millie's body is buried, we can hold her memories and love in our minds." It is a good idea to state that though people die, love doesn't ever die and you will always have their love; or, while every living thing dies, memories continue to thrive.

Will We See Him Again?

When a child asks if she will see her loved one again, the question is a little open-ended. Maybe she does not understand that death is final, or maybe she is asking if she will see Uncle Gabriel in an open casket at the funeral. Before assuming that you know what she is asking and answering with too much information, it would be better to ask for clarification.

"What do you mean? I'd like to answer your question, but can you tell me a little more?"

If your child means to ask whether she will see Uncle Gabriel for pizza as she used to on Wednesday evenings, then the answer might be, "We won't see Uncle Gabriel again because he isn't alive anymore, and so his body can't walk and talk now. It's very sad. But we can remember all the times we spent with him."

A question about an open casket could be answered simply, or if you don't know about funeral arrangements, you could tell your child you will find out and let her know. Then make sure you give her the information, as the knowledge will be reassuring. We talk more about funerals and after-death rituals in Chapter 9.

Very often, after the news has been broken, children don't know what they want to ask and so don't say anything. They may not have the skills to turn all the feelings or thoughts welling up inside them into a cogent question, and that is fine. Not everything has to be elaborated all at once. It is appropriate for you to let your child stay with his feelings inside, as long as you let him know that he can ask you questions later and that you remain attentive to his needs.

In later chapters, we provide tools for you to help your child articulate and understand the complex feelings he is having.

Anxiety may make it difficult for your child to take in fully the upsetting information. Be prepared to sit quietly with her in a loving and at least seemingly comfortable

TAKEAWAY

Times of sitting in attentive silence with your child may feel awkward, but they can give your child a moment to take in the news and help him feel less alone with his emotions.

way, allowing her the time and space to let the news percolate. It may be hard to process in the moment, but it is a gift to be present with your child in an empathic way when she is feeling sad, anxious, confused, or even angry. The message you want to convey is that you can tolerate her feelings, are willing to revisit the discussion over the course of time, and that it is not closed now that you have shared the news; it is an ongoing conversation.

How

It's best to try to be as calm as you can when talking with your child—though it may feel impossible. You may worry that you won't be able to deliver the news without becoming overwhelmed with emotion. We believe it's fine to cry and express feelings of sadness, as it models for children that it's natural to feel this way after someone dies. In general, we recommend trying to stay two shades less emotional than your child. We would say that tearing up, choking up, and crying are fine, but sobbing or wailing is likely to worry or frighten your child. If at any time during the conversation you feel uncontrollably anguished, it is better to excuse yourself for a moment so that your child doesn't feel overwhelmed. You might say, "I'm going to take a few minutes to let my feelings settle and then I'll be right back." Or the other adult in the room could say this for you if you can't get the words out. Either way, it's important for you to return to the conversation in a little while. If you are consistently distressed to the point where you can no longer speak coherently, it

> **TAKEAWAY**
>
> Be aware that sobbing and other strong displays of emotion may be hard for your child to handle, so, to the extent that you can, try to do your more intense crying in private.

may be better to say that you are feeling very sad, and then to leave and let the other adult continue. It is important for you to return to the conversation when you can.

As we noted in Chapter 3, be aware that children will take in both verbal and non-verbal information as you begin to communicate about a loss. They will be attuned to your affect, your external expression of emotions, and your energy, and these cues are often as powerful as the words you use. Children will absorb information in ways that you may not intend and may not be obvious from the language you choose to use. It can be especially confusing for children when a parent is saying one thing but their actions are expressing something else. If you are stating that you're fine while pacing around or nervously shredding a tissue, it sends a conflicting message that can worry your child. Some parents try to hide their sadness from their child, even delivering news of a death in a cheerful way, which again can lead to confusion. It is perfectly reasonable for you to express your sorrow in front of your child and, most helpful for them, to say, as you can, that while you are feeling down now you expect to feel better in a while.

We have provided the basic framework for you to be able to have an initial conversation with your child about the illness or death of a loved one. We will elaborate in later chapters on the nuances of such a discussion (including how to offer only as few details as necessary and how to handle your child's reactions), as well as provide guidelines for specific losses. However, we'd like to include one cardinal rule up front, as parents ask us this question very often: Is it okay to lie to protect children from knowing details that may be distressing? Our very clear position is that you should never lie—period. We will help you find comfortable enough ways to talk about the loss so that you will not feel the need to do so. In the next chapter, we address the subject of parents keeping secrets from their children, and the idea of telling the truth in a way that gives your child age-appropriate information.

One of Elena's patients, a sixteen-year-old boy, confided in his mother about having a crush. When Elena asked how he was able to feel at ease telling his parent, he said he'd always talked about everything with her, ever since he could remember. As he thought more about the question, he recalled her sitting him down when he was five years old and telling him about his beloved uncle Rafael's death. He also remembered when his soccer coach died, sitting in the kitchen with his mom, crying and asking questions. "My mom never lied to me," he said. "She thought I deserved the truth."

The willingness to have a conversation on a difficult topic can be a cornerstone of a parent-child relationship. In addition, modeled on the open and honest talks you have had with her over the years, as a child grows into a young adult she will be able to give time to inner reflection about how she feels and continue these conversations with herself and others. This is a wonderfully positive outcome. This willingness to hold space open for children to ask questions over the course of time and to receive truthful answers is an important kind of communication for parents, one that children notice, and one that engenders trust.

Chapter 6

Why Tell the Truth—
and How to Do It

Introducing Best Practices:
Don't keep secrets and *Tell the truth, nothing but the truth
but not necessarily the whole truth—at least not all at once*

✳ Honesty Is a Cornerstone of Parenting ✳

✳ Secrets Breed Worry and Confusion ✳

✳ Finding a Middle Ground in Telling the Truth ✳

✳ Tailoring Answers to Your Child's Needs ✳

✳ Handling Direct Questions ✳

✳ Talking About a Death That Preceded Your Child's Birth ✳

✳ Revisiting Conversations Over Time ✳

Many parents struggle with the idea of being completely honest with their children in conversations about illness and death. You might wonder how it is possible to be truthful about such upsetting subjects that seem far beyond the realm of what your child could possibly need to know. You may believe you are doing your child a favor by sheltering him from news you think too stark. Our aims in this chapter are to help you understand how your child can be eased by knowing the truth, and to furnish you with the skills to remain honest while balancing your comfort level—and your child's—with how much information to give.

When Darren was four, his father was burned in an explosion at work and rushed to the emergency room. Darren's mother, Lisa, explained that Daddy had been hurt and would spend some time in the hospital where doctors could help to make him better. Over the next weeks, Lisa managed to keep Darren's routine as regular as possible, dropping him at day care each morning and having her sister watch him in the evening while she visited the hospital. Even so, he became clingy, begging his mother not to leave him. One night he awoke and sobbed about a fire, saying he was scared it was going to get him like it got Daddy. Lisa was surprised. She hadn't mentioned the fire to him, thinking it would frighten him.

The next day Darren was scheduled to have his first meeting with Michael to help him navigate his father's hospitalization and the long weeks of recovery that might lie ahead. Lisa mentioned Darren's fear of the fire. As Michael spoke to the little boy, it turned out he had heard Lisa talking about the accident with her sister.

"She said there was a big bang—boom!—and fire," Darren told him. "Fire everywhere." His eyes were wide with fear.

It became clear to Michael that Darren had been worrying about the fire for a while and trying to understand it on his own. He thought it was still burning, unchecked and dangerous. Lisa's omission had left room for Darren to create his own narrative, one that terrified him. During their initial meeting and several others that week, Darren was able to talk openly with Michael about his fears and to understand that firefighters had extinguished the fire and it could not hurt anyone else.

Unfortunately, the next week Darren's father's condition took a sudden downward turn. Infection overwhelmed his lungs, and he died. Lisa and her sister were devastated and it was decided that Michael was the person best equipped to give Darren the news, with Lisa present. Later that afternoon, mother and son came for the therapy session, and Michael settled Darren in. After a few minutes he said he had some sad news to share, then said simply that Darren's father had died.

"He's in the hospital," said Darren. "He'll be home soon."

Michael said he was sorry but the doctors had not been able to make his father better. Darren began to cry.

"It is very sad news," said Michael. He sat with Darren, giving him space to let his feelings out, while Lisa wept quietly. As the tears subsided, they sat in silence for a few more minutes until Michael asked, "Do you have any questions?"

Darren nodded. "Why couldn't the doctors fix him?"

It was a question that Michael had anticipated. The father had suffered severe burns and died of multi-organ failure brought on by a blood infection. Michael wanted to be honest but he also wanted to avoid unnecessary details. He told Darren that the smoke had hurt his father's lungs and that they had stopped working. The little boy nodded. He didn't have any more questions. Michael had told the truth by choosing which details to leave out.

In the previous chapter, we created a framework to ease you into an initial conversation with your child to share news of a serious illness or death that would have an impact on his world. We emphasized the need to keep the exchange simple and to not provide too many details. Here we underscore and expand upon that advice by introducing two best practices that will help you make your way through both the initial and subsequent conversations: 1) *Don't keep secrets*, and 2) *Tell the truth, nothing but the truth but not necessarily the whole truth—at least not all at once.* Often they work hand in hand, providing you with a safe way through conversations riddled with what can seem like a minefield of potential parent pitfalls. Honesty is crucial in relationships with children and especially so when talking about the serious illness or loss of a loved one. Parents of young children are laying important groundwork for communication with their child now and into the future. Lying to them, downplaying, or hiding information is a breach of trust that may reverberate in the parent-child relationship in powerful and harmful ways. Now and going forward, you want your child to know that what you say is reliable and true and that you are willing to be honest even when the truth is upsetting or uncomfortable. This will establish a pattern for those later years when your child may become more secretive and rule challenging. She may be more inclined to hide a truth from you if you have been dishonest with her. And, on the flip side, she is more likely to come to you to talk through difficult subjects if you have laid a foundation of trust during her childhood.

Don't Keep Secrets

First let's consider the best practice *Don't keep secrets.*

As the news of the terrorist attacks unfolded on the morning of September 11, 2001, Elena and her husband thought they were doing a good job of avoiding all mention of it in front of their not quite three-year-old son, Solomon. They wanted him to learn about the news when they knew enough to explain it to him clearly. That afternoon, however, he went straight to his basket of blocks and set about building several tall towers. Next he knocked them down with his helicopter toy. Elena realized all over again how difficult it is to keep secrets from children no matter how hard you try.

In a similar situation, early in the COVID-19 pandemic, the three-year-old sibling of one of Michael's patients put tissue masks on all her stuffed animals and hid under her bed with them. "We don't want to get sick!" she said. Despite the family's attempt to keep the news of the pandemic from her, she had clearly figured out on her own some version of what was going on in the world.

In Darren's case, his mother kept secrets from him about his father's accident. She had many reasons for doing so. She was going through unspeakable emotional trauma herself as she dealt with her husband's sudden injury, and she thought that she was doing the right thing by sparing her young son the details. This desire to protect our children from the truth is a common parent pitfall, as we have previously seen. No matter how hard we try to keep the truth from our children, no matter how good our intentions, they will almost always figure it out. Either in an overt way, such as hearing adults talking when they think their child is out of earshot, or by stumbling upon an email or text message. Or a child might find out in a more abstract way, noticing perhaps that emotional currents have changed, that a parent is tearful, distracted, impatient, or absent from home more. He may hear whispered conversations and wonder about multiple phone calls, sensing that something big is happening in his small world.

TAKEAWAY

Even when you are overwhelmed yourself, there are ways to tell your child the truth.

Keeping secrets can take many forms. It might be a deliberate decision on the part of a parent to not tell a child about an illness or death in the hope that she hasn't heard or won't figure out that an important emotional event is unfolding around her. For example, maybe a distant relative, one the child rarely sees, has a terminal illness, or a member of his school community has died, someone he didn't personally know, or the news of a mass shooting is playing out in the media. Parents may decide that in these cases there is no need for their child to be informed. Many parents feel the same way about deaths that preceded their child's birth, thinking that these past deaths will have no effect on their child going forward. We will show you later in this chapter how this is not the case. These secrets can be seen as acts of omission. Sometimes parents might engage in a more nuanced skirting of the truth. They may plan on telling their child about an illness or death in the family, but by delaying the conversation too long they inadvertently turn the information into a secret and withhold the truth.

We know that parents mean well when they keep secrets from their children, but in our experience children suffer when the truth is hidden. They become anxious and insecure. Although they may not have the language to articulate their feelings, they understand when there is something significant or painful happening in the lives of their parents, even when they are not explicitly told. Being closed out of that experience or having parents pretend that everything is "fine" worries them. Trying to keep secrets around serious illness or death often has the unintended effect of leaving children entirely alone with complex feelings they don't understand. Even if the news is very difficult, your child might create even worse imaginings of what is going on that cause additional fear and anxiety. When children have to handle their worries on their own, it's the difference between being afraid of the dark alone versus being in the dark with someone else, which makes it much less scary.

Sometimes parents share with their child news of a death or a serious illness but are not completely forthcoming about the details. Perhaps they say that Grandma is sick but don't feel comfortable explaining to a child that the illness is terminal and she will die, thus delaying the bad news. We speak more on this in Chapter 10.

Sometimes parents keep secrets about the cause of death. They may believe it will scare a child to hear when someone has died in an accident, or in a violent way, or by suicide, and so prefer to tell their child an untruth.

Forty-five-year-old Sherry, one of Elena's patients, was devastated when her older sister Ginny suffered a heart attack while swimming and drowned. Sherry knew that her sister had a chronic heart condition and wondered if ocean swimming had been too much for her. Though Sherry told her seven-year-old son, Robbie, about the death, she couldn't bring herself to tell him about the drowning. She thought he might become fearful around water. Instead, she told him only that his aunt had suffered a heart attack. A few weeks later, Robbie heard the truth from his older cousins and was understandably confused. Sherry told Elena how sad she had felt to see the muddled expression on his face when he came to her and asked if Aunt Ginny had drowned.

"I told him I was worried the news might upset him," Sherry said to Elena.

"What did he say?" asked Elena.

"He said, 'You lied to me, Mommy.'" Sherry paused. "And he was right."

Later, Robbie did start to worry about drowning. Sherry's lie had made him anxious and confused to the point that he felt being around water was something that he *should* be concerned about. Just the fact that it had been kept secret made it seem like something too terrible to talk about. He refused to go to his swimming lessons and stayed far from the ocean when his family went on a weekend trip to the beach. He didn't know what to do about his feelings and didn't feel comfortable telling his mother. She was no longer as trustworthy in his eyes. Finally, when he started having nightmares in which he was drowning and woke up gasping for breath, Sherry brought him to see Elena and he began to process his fears.

After getting to know Robbie, and working with him over time, Elena was able to talk to him in a truthful way by using details that were appropriate for his age. She acknowledged his fears about drowning, and agreed that sometimes people died by drowning just as his aunt Ginny had done. She also reassured him that drowning deaths happened rarely and that there were ways to reduce the risks for him, such as continuing his swimming lessons and going in the water with an adult until he felt more comfortable. When she spoke with Robbie's mother, she advised, "Keep talking with Robbie. Accept his questions and shape your answers to his needs. Be truthful."

Tell the Truth

Our recommendation to not keep secrets from your child does not mean that you should give her every detail. Instead, there is a middle ground.

We advise combining the best practice *Don't keep secrets* with *Tell the truth, nothing but the truth but not necessarily the whole truth—at least not all at once.* In conversations with young children, begin with simple, basic information and stay attuned to your

> **TAKEAWAY**
> By telling the truth you prevent mistrust from your child, because he will almost always eventually find out secrets or lies about a death.

child and the specific questions she is asking (or not asking). What additional information is she seeking? A child does not need to know all the details of an accident or an illness if she asks the question of how Grandma died. "She had a sickness that stopped her lungs from working anymore" is an honest and complete answer. There is no need to mention the wrenching decision to take Grandma off life support, even if it is the main thing on your mind. "He hurt his head very badly when his car crashed into a tree" is enough information for a young child to understand why her uncle is in the hospital and may die. The fact that he had been driving while intoxicated is not something she needs to know (though it may be something to explain in more detail if she ever asks or as she grows older).

When Elena's son built towers out of wooden blocks and knocked them down, she realized that he had absorbed news about the terrorist attacks on the Twin Towers. Clearly the event was on his mind and he was looking to find a way to process it. Kneeling on the floor with Solomon as he played, Elena opened up a conversation about buildings falling down and was able to speak with him on the subject in an age-appropriate way. Her aim was to give him the space to form questions that she would answer with the truth.

Later that day, as he was getting ready for bed, Solomon suddenly asked, "Why did it happen?"

"You mean, about the buildings getting knocked down?"

He nodded. He had undoubtedly been pondering the subject since the earlier conversation.

"Some people flew the planes into the buildings on purpose because they were so angry at some people in our country and wanted to hurt them. There are less hurtful ways to show how mad you are and it's very sad it happened like this."

She explained that the police and all sorts of other people in charge were finding out more to make sure that it didn't happen again. At that, he nodded and clambered into bed, ready for his usual bedtime stories.

Our aim in sharing these best practices is to show that there are always ways to speak to your child, even about the most devastating news. Finding simple words to tell the truth helps young children to understand what has happened, to begin to sort out their reactions, and to process the pain with your help. An explanation tailored to their needs reassures children rather than worrying them. When told the truth, they do not need to fear the unknown, or imagine and invent possible scenarios based on snippets of conversations or distortions.

Sometimes children may ask questions that catch parents off guard, and formulating an answer that is honest while not revealing more than necessary can be difficult in the moment. If you experience that very common "deer in the headlights" feeling, it is perfectly reasonable to say something like, "I am so glad you asked that but I'm not sure of the answer. I will figure it out and talk with you about it tomorrow after lunch." Then of course the question needs to be discussed after lunch the next day. Every question does not need to be answered on the spot, and you can always take time to think (and maybe to consult a trusted resource), as long as you circle back with a response.

Some questions asked by children, especially by the very young child, can be piercingly direct and may cause a parent unintended but real emotional pain. In this case, it is okay to tell your child that you want to answer her question but that you may need a few moments—or longer—as you'd like to gather your thoughts. The message you want to send is that asking all questions is acceptable even if they bring up negative feelings. You don't want your child to internalize that talking about loss will make you or other adults feel bad, as they will learn to "clam up" in order to protect you.

Common Questions

How Do You Know When You're Dead?

We would suggest an answer along the lines of: "When people die, all feelings and thoughts and body functions stop, so they aren't able to wonder if they are dead or not." Or "Some people believe that people who are dead go to a special place and when they arrive they are told that they have died."

Does It Hurt When You Die?

Instead of getting into a conversation about different causes of death and relative pain levels, we suggest: "When you die, all pain stops."

Where Is Grandpa Now?

"His body is buried in the churchyard, but I keep thoughts and memories of him with me." Or answer according to your beliefs. "I think he is in a place called heaven," or "He's in paradise, free of pain."

Will I Die of a Heart Attack, Too, Just like Aunt Toni?

"It isn't possible to catch a heart attack like you can a cold or the flu, so you don't have to worry about that. Your doctor listens to your heart every checkup and has always said your heart is very healthy."

What Is Suicide?

We answer many questions about suicide in Chapter 11 and provide suggestions for helping children to understand suicide as a disease.

All these answers are honest and speak to a young child's level of understanding. They seek to tell the truth and to reassure.

Jonathan was in his late twenties when he came to see Elena after the death of his mother. His father had died a few years earlier, and Jonathan had recently cleared out his mother's house, his childhood home, to put it on the market. He had been stunned to find baby clothes, photographs, and a death certificate in a box in the basement. It turned out that his parents had a daughter who had died at the age of two a few years before Jonathan was born. Now he felt like his entire childhood had been turned upside down, that he had to rethink everything, and was angry that his parents had kept a secret from him about something that was so monumental to them. His parents likely didn't tell him about his sister's death to protect him from feelings of fear and sadness—and to protect themselves from facing their unbearable loss again—and now they were no longer alive to be able to process his sister's (life and) death with him. They would probably have been horrified to understand how much their instinctive and well-meaning actions had hurt and damaged their adult son.

In contrast, Elijah and Dyani came to see Michael for help in speaking with their five-year-old daughter, Leilani. Eighteen months before Leilani was born, they had suffered through the heartbreaking experience of delivering a stillborn son. They had named the baby Kye, after their love of the ocean in their native Hawaii, and planted a tree in his memory. When Leilani was born, Elijah and Dyani included her in their visits to the tree and, as she grew older, they let her hang ribbons in the branches. They had told her that the tree was planted for her brother, but they had never really explained what had happened to him. Recently, Leilani had said she didn't want to go to the tree, that it was silly. She had also started wetting the bed and her preschool teacher had called to say that she had pinched one of her classmates and scribbled on his artwork. It turned out that he had told Leilani that she didn't have a brother.

Elijah and Dyani needed help in explaining, as they put it, how to tell a five-year-old about the death of a baby. It was hard for them to return to their painful experience and to understand why Leilani needed to know. Michael helped the couple to view the world through their daughter's eyes, and they began to see that it was a confusing place. When she asked questions about Kye's death, her parents told her what she already knew, and the space between her questions and her knowledge began to fill with scary ideas.

With a new understanding that an honest conversation, one that told the truth without going into unnecessary details, would benefit Leilani, her parents made the brave decision to tell her what had happened to Kye. It was the beginning of a new way of communicating with her, one that would bring them all closer.

As children grow and their understanding of the world expands, the simple conversations and explanations they were told when they were very young may be revisited. As Elena's son matured, she and her husband had multiple conversations with him about the events of September 11, each one tapered toward where he was in his development at the time. Darren learned more about his father's death as he grew older, each telling unpeeling another layer of the onion, but not one contradicted the initial version that contained all the truth he had needed as a four-year-old.

As you learn the best practices *Don't keep secrets* and *Tell the truth, nothing but the truth but not necessarily the whole truth—at least not all at once*, you'll begin to feel comfortable finding your way through difficult conversations. You may even discover that they are not as challenging as you first anticipated and may begin to embrace the opportunity they offer as they arise. No matter what, your courage in committing to telling your child the truth is a gift to them, one that will prove beneficial to you both now and in the years to come.

Chapter 7

Your Child's Reaction—Keeping an Open Mind

Introducing Best Practices:
Know your child and *Expect the unexpected*

✳ Your Child Is Unique ✳ Validating All Responses ✳
✳ Easing Feelings of Guilt ✳ Considering How Your Child
Might Respond ✳ When Things Don't Go According to Plan ✳
✳ "No Reaction" Is a Reaction ✳ Staying Calm ✳
✳ The Power of Sitting in Silence ✳ Attentive Listening ✳

Parents are often uncomfortable with the idea of telling a child about illness or death because they are worried about how he might respond to the news. Many parents have said to us, "I just can't tell my child. I won't know how to handle her reaction." Or "I can't bear to hear his crying, not on top of everything else." Whether a child is likely to greet the news with a lot of outward emotion or none at all, parents are often afraid that they won't have the skills to handle such reactions and find themselves paralyzed by the very idea of trying. While we understand these parental concerns, it is best to work through them nonetheless, to be able to give your child difficult news. We can't tell you exactly how your child will respond, but we can help you to be available for whatever your child's particular reaction looks like. In that way, you can feel ready to meet any and all responses with thought and care to lovingly support your child.

First, remember that every child is unique, and that means that responses to breaking the news will come in many different ways. When telling siblings together—which we recommend—be aware that children in the same family can have very different reactions to the same situation. A five-year-old may burst into tears, while his eight-year-old sister covers her ears and refuses to speak. Some children have lots of questions and some only want to know whether they can go play with their cars. It is crucial to show that you accept all reactions to a loss in a caring way. Just because one child cried and the other continued to play with her puzzle, it doesn't mean that the one who outwardly showed his sadness loved his aunt more.

Many parents are surprised to find that children express emotions other than unhappiness around sad news, and it's important to convey that all feelings are okay to have. Some children may be confused or feel guilty if they don't immediately cry or feel sad, especially if parents seem to be suggesting that they should. The pause we recommend after sharing hard news with children is one in which they can find their reaction, whatever it may be. You can explain that tears or sorrow may come later or not at all—that everyone grieves for loved ones in different ways. The memories of the person they lost are still inside them even if they don't have a sad reaction, and they can remember them whenever they like. Sometimes anger may be the preliminary reaction, aimed at the person who died or at others who didn't prevent the death. Instead of shutting it down, allow your child space for her feelings and sit with her, then ask what is making her angry and hear her out. It may be her way of expressing feelings of vulnerability about being left by someone dying, and can be easily misunderstood. As grief involves all our emotions, it makes sense that anger occurs in its processing. Some children show embarrassment in school for being the center of attention after a death, while others may relish it and try to prolong it. Let your child know that all these feelings are natural responses, and that she can handle each one with you by her side.

It can be common for children to believe that they are responsible for a death, and they may ask, "Was it my fault?" Elena remembers wondering at the age of five whether she had caused her aunt to die because she didn't enjoy visiting her on Sundays and would have preferred not to do so. Was her aunt's death an answer to her wish? It is developmentally appropriate for young children to have a sense of omnipotence, and this may lead to thoughts such as, "Did I make my cat sick because I was mad she scratched me?" or "Did our neighbor die because I didn't want him to come over for Thanksgiving?"

These thoughts can bring feelings of guilt and confusion, adding an extra layer of complexity to a child's reactions to a death. Michael worked with a family to help them process the sudden death of their babysitter, a young woman in her twenties who had died in a car accident. One of the children, six-year-old Poppy, became withdrawn, finding it difficult to talk about her babysitter and having nightmares that wakened her most nights. It turned out that she thought the death was her fault.

"I was mad at her for winning at Go Fish," she told Michael. "I called her names and wished she wasn't my babysitter anymore."

Later, when Michael spoke with Poppy's parents, he explained that she was feeling guilty about what had happened. He encouraged them to talk to Poppy about her worries, to let her know she was not responsible for the death, to help her understand that angry interchanges can occur naturally in relationships, and to encourage her to think of what she could do now to feel better.

It's valuable for a child to know that her connection to a person is the sum of all the connections she had to him, and that it's not all about the very last one or a particularly unkind one. This knowledge eases a child's guilt—as it does for parents, too—when her last interaction with the person who died was not a good one.

Poppy's parents helped her to write a letter as if it were for her babysitter, saying she was sorry that she had called her a name and that she had loved having her as her babysitter. Next Poppy started to write a list of fun things they had done together—building a fort, going sledding, taking the bus to the beach—and as she did so she was able to see how much more there was to their relationship than that one last encounter.

> **TAKEAWAY**
>
> A person's link to someone who has died arises from all their prior connections with them, not just the final one, so an angry last interaction does not destroy their connection.

Know Your Child

While a child's reaction to the news of a death may feel like uncharted territory, there are some ways for you to prepare. We believe the best practice *Know your child* will be helpful here. It runs parallel to *Know your own thoughts and feelings*, introduced in Chapter 3, and just as you have considered your own reactions to a death before telling your child so as to be aware of, and address, your own vulnerabilities first, it is useful now to turn your attention to how your child is likely to respond.

This is a time to think empathically, considering your child's needs above your own and contemplating what he will need from you in responding to this loss. You may come to realize that you previously had a conversation in mind, one that reflected your own expectations of how to deliver the news rather than how your child would likely receive it. Taking the time to anticipate how your child tends to react to challenging situations and how he may best be helped through the experience is a vital part of the process. It will likely help you feel more grounded going into a conversation.

HOW DOES YOUR CHILD DEAL WITH SEPARATION AND LOSS IN GENERAL?

o   How has he reacted to prior losses or upsets?

HOW DOES YOUR CHILD DEAL WITH BIG EMOTIONS?

o   Does he tend to talk about his feelings or withdraw?

o   Is he more inclined to enact his feelings physically or emotionally (stomping, crying) in the moment, or is he likely to bury his feelings until a later time?

HOW HAVE YOU HELPED YOUR CHILD WITH INTENSE FEELINGS IN THE PAST?

o   What has worked for him?

o   Will he want physical closeness or prefer some space after hearing the news?

o Will he want to occupy his mind with toys or books or other activities?

HOW DOES THIS LOSS CHANGE YOUR CHILD'S LIFE?

o Did he feel close to the person?

o How might that affect his response?

o Did he see them on a regular basis?

When Things Don't Go According to Plan

It is possible that your predictions about your child's responses will not be accurate, or not entirely so, and we recommend that you keep another best practice in mind: *Expect the unexpected.* Be open to any reactions your child might have. In some ways, this advice may seem daunting, but, in our experience, it can be helpful to acknowledge that some of this process is beyond your control. In doing so, you can prepare yourself for how to stay with your child emotionally when he surprises you. Even with the best preparation, every parent faces times when they don't know what to do, in both happy and sad situations. It is part of the package of caring for children. No matter your child's reaction, anticipated or not, it is useful to remind yourself to try to stay calm, patient, and compassionate. If you feel yourself becoming overwrought or angry, take a minute to catch your breath. It will help you and your child.

One of Michael's patients talked about his five-year-old son's surprising response to the death of his beloved grandmother. When young Henry was given the news, he slipped off the couch and started to build with his Legos. His dad asked if he had any questions, but he didn't say a word.

"He's just been going about his days as usual. I thought he was going to cry and cry," the father said. "I thought he really loved his grandma. He cried more when his hamster died."

Michael explained that this "no reaction" response was Henry's way of reacting. Perhaps he didn't have the words to express just how much his small world had been rocked by the loss of someone so important to him, or maybe he had questions that he was unable to frame. Parents can mistakenly believe that if a child doesn't ask questions, then he doesn't have any. Or that if he doesn't show any emotions, he's not experiencing any. By staying attuned to your child's needs, you can continue to offer him time and space so that he feels loved and secure and can express his emotions when he is ready.

A few days later, Henry's father decided to read *Goodnight Moon*, one of Henry and his grandma's favorite books. As Henry listened, he started crying, then said, through tears, "I miss Grandma."

Just as Henry's father learned that "no reaction" is a valid reaction, he realized that he had assumed his son's response would "match" the circumstances of his loss, that his love for his grandma would translate into an extreme reaction to her death. It is not always possible to anticipate what kind of reaction will be set in motion.

With Elena's help, Alina and Bartek had worked out a plan for letting their children know that Bartek's father had died. They had talked about the best words to use and had considered how their children would react. Four-year-old Sasha would cry, they thought, and would want to be held. Seven-year-old Theo would likely say nothing and would probably draw or build something and think things through.

However, when they told their children the sad news, things didn't go quite as expected. Sasha welled up with tears and moved to snuggle with her father, while Theo stood up and started stomping around. Bartek and Alina exchanged glances. They weren't sure what to do. Alina got to her feet and walked with her son as he continued to stomp around the room. Wordlessly, Theo took her hand and marched past the sofa and back, leading his mother with him. Then he let go of her hand, stomped toward his dad and sat down on the floor across from him. "Did it hurt Grandpa when he died?" he asked.

Bartek blinked a little. He didn't want to think about whether his father had suffered. The question—along with the stomping—was uncharacteristic of Theo, definitely part of the "expect the unexpected" that Elena had mentioned. Bartek looked toward his wife and she kneeled down next to their son.

"I'm glad you asked your question. Grandpa was in some pain but the doctors worked hard to help it go away."

Alina and Bartek used the best practice *Know your child* ahead of breaking the news to Theo and Sasha and anticipated their likely reactions. They also used the best practice *Expect the unexpected*. This helped them to respond thoughtfully and lovingly to Theo's surprising behavior, which should be a parent's primary aim. Try to allow your child to have her reaction without having the same reaction yourself so that you can support her through her response in a balanced way. Sometimes parents take on or mirror their child's emotions and it can bring an additional layer of intensity to a situation. By being aware of your role ahead of time, it may be easier to tend to your child's needs, come what may.

What might have happened if Alina and Bartek had tried to prevent Theo's natural response, telling him to sit down and stop his stomping? Based on our experience, we think his angry feelings might have escalated and the stomping could have turned into a full-scale tantrum. Alternatively, he could have stopped stomping, rushed back to join his family in the circle, and slunk down in shame, probably shutting down his emotions for the rest of the discussion. Either way, he would have felt that his reaction was not acceptable.

It may not always be possible or easy to remain levelheaded in the face of your child's reactions. If you find you are caught off guard or respond in a way you later regret, you can always revisit those moments with your child.

"Yesterday, I got mad at you for stomping when you heard the news that Grandpa had died. I'm sorry. I shouldn't have done that. It was okay for you to have those feelings and to let me know."

In fact, being able to think about an earlier interaction and to tell your child that you want to say or do something different is an important relationship tool to model and an essential part of your child building her own capacity for reflection.

One of Elena's friends was able to revisit a comment she made to her granddaughter. When four-year-old Bella's guinea pig died, she was inconsolable, refusing to eat her lunch and throwing herself on the floor when it was time to go to preschool. In exasperation, her grandmother said, "Oh, for goodness' sake, Bella, it was just a guinea pig! You can get another one." This only brought on another wave of tears from Bella. Immediately, Grandma knew she'd said the wrong thing and realized she hadn't acknowledged Bella's grief over the loss of her pet and had invalidated her reaction. It was time for a do-over.

For many children, the death of a pet is their first experience with loss. It is a time for parents to value the expression of feelings of any kind, to give their child time and space to find their reactions, and to support them through their loss. This important lesson will apply to all subsequent deaths—animal or human—that a child will experience during her life.

TAKEAWAY

The death of a pet can be an important early opportunity to help your child learn about handling loss.

When a child can recognize his own feelings and knows he can express them to trusted people, then he is developing skills that will help him to communicate and process emotions effectively as he grows up.

Sometimes a child's reactions to a death may be difficult to hear. Perhaps they say they're happy that someone died because that person was mean to them or was always angry. Again, it's important to accept these feelings instead of judging them. You can point out that you understand that your child is happy she won't have to experience certain actions or situations anymore while stating that it's sad that the person in question isn't alive anymore. By being open and ready to try to understand, to put yourself in your child's shoes in an empathic way, you will find you can handle even the most unexpected reactions.

We are strong advocates of sitting in silence with a child as he expresses and processes emotions. We find that parents often want to fix their child's sadness/anxiety/confusion/anger, or whatever is their response to a challenging situation, and when they can't they feel helpless. However, just sitting with a child and staying connected to him as he experiences significant emotions and moves through different feeling states is in itself a very good way of helping.

Attentive listening and being aware of your child's emotional pain sends a message of support that you, his parent, are willing to accept, acknowledge, and be with him in his discomfort. You are modeling that both having and expressing a range of feelings is okay. This will allow your child in his other relationships now, and for years to come, to be able to develop

TAKEAWAY
Bearing witness is healing and helps your child know she is not alone with her emotions.

deep, authentic, and enduring connections with friends, family, and partners.

This active and open listening combined with a willingness to meet your child's responses—whatever they may be—with compassion will provide you with the confidence to manage any emotional terrain. These skills are essential as your child hears upsetting news and traverses difficult situations throughout his childhood, both related to loss and not. It's helpful to remember that reactions may occur long after the immediate death, brought on by anniversaries, birthdays, places, or other remembrances that seem to appear simply out of the blue. You will be able to use your new tools to help your child to navigate each time by validating and listening—and over the years he will absorb and take on these skills for himself.

Chapter 8

Name the Experience: What's Mentionable Is Manageable

Introducing Best Practice:
Name the experience

✳ The Power of Verbalizing the Inner Experience ✳

✳ Tools to Develop Emotional Awareness ✳ Acknowledging Confusion ✳

✳ Navigating Emotions Around Illness and Death ✳

✳ Using the Creative Arts to Name Feelings ✳

✳ Developing Empathy, Connection, and Grit ✳

The news of serious illness or death can bring heightened reactions, and the ability to recognize these emotions and to know how to respond effectively to them, in the moment and over time, is invaluable for both adults and children. Learning about loss opens your child up to a lot of different thoughts and feelings, and we have recommended that you be receptive to all of them. In this chapter, we add another layer to the process by introducing the best practice *Name the experience* to help you understand and feel comfortable with the vital role that emotions play in your child's life, especially as he learns to navigate difficult situations. You may be surprised to hear that, while your child's emotional responses to upsetting news may be many and varied, he might have limited understanding of what his feelings mean, much less how to cope. The knowledge of the illness or death of a loved one may bring with it emotions that are completely new to him, or that may be more intense than usual, or are wrapped up with other emotions in complicated ways. With *Name the experience*, we provide you with tools to help your child recognize his emotions, a powerful skill that will connect him to himself and help him relate empathically to others in a useful and positive way. It will bolster him as he hears distressing news for the first time, and as he continues to process it over the days, months, and even years to come. This ability to put words to feelings promotes communication—and resolution—and while we use it here to navigate emotions around illness and death, we think you may find it extremely beneficial in many areas of parenting as your child experiences strong feelings about major as well as more minor moments in his life.

Finding the Words for a Feeling

Michael's patient Jeff struggled when his wife died unexpectedly. Overwhelmed by the loss and his sole responsibility for Renée, their six-year-old daughter, he found it hard to function. He was also concerned about Renée, who was quiet, withdrawn, and alone in her grief. He didn't seem able to reach her.

"Does she cry?" asked Michael. "Or say she misses her mother?"

"No," said Jeff, "or at least not in front of me. She used to like to read to me, but she's stopped, and she doesn't see her friends much. I'm not sure how to help."

Together, he and Michael came up with a plan and on the weekend Jeff was able to carry it out. After breakfast, he brought out paper and markers and settled at the kitchen table with Renée. In the past she would have started drawing, but now she just sat. Jeff started on a picture, drawing swirls of light and dark blue, then added purple and black until his page was filled with an ominous thundercloud. "That's how I'm feeling inside," he said. "Angry. And confused, too." Renée watched as he added drops of rain in blue marker. "Some days I just want to cry," he said. "Feeling like you don't want to talk or play can be a way of feeling sad." He looked up at Renée. "I wonder if you might be feeling sad, too." She picked up a marker, and started to draw. She filled her piece of paper from edge to edge in just one color. An ocean of gray. "I feel sad all over," she said.

Sometimes when children experience emotions, they don't know how to describe in words what is happening in their minds and this can be upsetting for them. Renée was overcome by powerful feelings after her mother's death and had withdrawn from her life in the face of them, until her father helped her to identify what she felt as sadness. Just finding the name for one part of the tangle of confusion inside made it seem less overwhelming. Once she understood it as sadness and

TAKEAWAY

Intense emotions can be confusing for young children, and your help will ease their discomfort with them.

could communicate that to her father, she was able to tolerate it as a named thing and begin to process it. Next she and her father would be able to look for ways to relieve her sorrow.

Naming an experience can help your child begin to handle difficult or painful feelings. Another way to think of this best practice is "What is mentionable is manageable." By naming the internal experience (for example, a feeling of anger), your child is able to feel the emotion and observe it at the same time, to bring the emotion out and connect it with her thoughts. She will start to associate a particular inner experience with a particular emotion and say, "When I feel like this, that means I'm sad," or "I know that feeling. I'm getting mad!" This does not make your child's feelings disappear (and that is good), but it does mean that she will be able to take steps to handle them, first by opening herself up to receiving an empathic response from you or other trusted people by asking for help ("I'm so mad!"), and, as she gets older and more experienced, by turning to what has worked for her in managing an emotion in the past.

TAKEAWAY

When your child can name her feelings, she can communicate and be understood more easily.

Identifying Emotions as a Parenting Tool

You may be surprised to learn that there are thousands of different emotions. Scientific research has diverged over the years on the number of "basic" ones, but it would be fair to say the most common are sadness, anger, happiness, and fear. Your child might refer to them as sad, mad, glad, and scared. When they are combined with another feeling or feelings, the emotional possibilities are endless. Given the sheer number and nuance, it is easy to see why many adults struggle to recognize and name their own feelings— and what to do in response to them—and understandable that children often require parental support and guidance in this area.

TAKEAWAY

Mad, sad, glad, and scared are the basic words you can use to help your children name their feelings.

We devote much of our time to helping our patients to make sense of their feelings and work constructively with them in response to many situations in their lives, and especially when they are experiencing events that have intensified their emotions. We believe that the ability to effectively access and handle emotions is key to understanding ourselves, our actions, and our relationships, and we explore here different ways for you to develop your child's emotional awareness in general before looking specifically at reactions around illness and death.

As a parent, you play a crucial role in narrating your young child's experience as he grows. From the time he was an infant, you have put words to basic feeling states: "You look like you are happy with that big smile on your face!" "I see your frown. Maybe you're feeling mad?" When your child hears you label your own feelings—"I am feeling frustrated," "I am feeling proud"—it helps him to make the connection between the emotions and the words. There are many ways for you to develop your child's understanding of emotions so that he can recognize feelings when they arise inside.

You could look for opportunities during daily activities to offer your child names for emotions she is showing so that she can learn to identify them.

You might say, "I know you wanted to go to the park today but we can't because it's raining. I see your tears and wonder if you are feeling sad?" Or, "I know you wanted to stay up late with your sisters but it was your bedtime. When you threw the pillow at me, do you think you may have been feeling mad?"

Give your child the opportunity to say what he thinks other people might be feeling.

"Grandma missed the bus so she won't be able to have lunch with us today. How do you think she feels about that?" Perhaps your child would answer, "Sad. I bet she's sad she won't get to see us." If you ask your child how *he* feels about the situation, he might say, "Sad, too. I like it when Grandma visits." Or maybe, "I'm mad at Grandma. Now we can't play Uno!" In this way, he will begin to see that the same situation can elicit different responses in different people. Or your child might be feeling both sad and mad. And maybe ashamed for feeling mad at Grandma. With just this one simple example, you can see how complex feelings can be.

As you attune yourself to your child's emotions, you enable him to feel seen and heard. When you guide him in understanding what his feelings are telling him, you move him along to the next step: how to handle emotions in effective ways. We will discuss this further in Chapter 9.

Emotional Responses to Difficult News

On breaking the news of an illness or death to your young child, she will experience an emotional reaction of some kind but may not know what the emotion is. In addition, she may feel many different things at once, and may find herself unable to convey what she is feeling inside. Sometimes too many feelings can overwhelm a child and make her shut down or throw a tantrum. It can be comforting for your child if you can help her to understand what confusion is, and that it is a common experience for both children and adults. You might say something like, "I think you may be having a lot of big feelings. When we're reacting to something new and we aren't sure what it is we feel, we call that being confused. It can feel like a lot of whirling in your mind, or a lot of not knowing."

TAKEAWAY

You can teach your child how to recognize when he feels confused.

If your child says he is experiencing confusion, your reassurance enables him to tolerate this uncomfortable feeling and to learn that it will fade over time as other emotions rise up. If you sit with him and give him a little time instead of rushing in to fix it, he can start to sort it out himself within the comfort of your presence. As time passes after breaking the news, and over the hours that follow, you might say, "Let's see if we can figure out why you're feeling confused and make sense of it." You could offer your child a feeling that he might be having in response to a death: "Sometimes people feel sad. Do you think you're feeling sad?" We recommend that parents not ask such questions one after the other but instead sprinkle them into moments of togetherness if your child brings up the loss. Too many questions at once can make your child shut down, so if your child begins to close off, it's a sign to stop for now.

Sometimes parents are concerned that they might cause their child to feel a certain way by imposing possible feelings. "I don't want him to feel scared so I won't suggest that he is." But you needn't be. Your child will reject a feeling that doesn't seem to fit if you offer it as an option, especially if you have asked the question in an open-ended way, such as, "Is it possible that you are . . . ?" If your child says he isn't feeling an emotion that you suggest, then accept his answer and leave it there. Don't push through, even if you are convinced he is feeling a certain way—there are always other opportunities to help to name that emotion with him. Once you help your child to identify the whirl of emotions inside, he can start to realize that he can do something about them.

Just as feelings can be interwoven in an overwhelming mass, they can also be layered. One of Michael's patients, four-year-old Archie, didn't cry after his grandfather's death and seemed angry instead. When his mom asked if he was upset about Grandpa, he said he was glad that his grandfather had died. His mom was distressed to hear this and her first thought was, "What a terrible thing to say!" but she kept it to herself and asked Archie why he felt that way. It turned out that he hadn't liked his mom going to visit Grandpa in the hospital. On hearing that, Archie's mom was able to say, "I think the happiness you're feeling is relief that I'll be home with you now. I know it's been hard for you to have me away so much. Though I'm very sad about Grandpa, I'm glad, too, that we can spend more time together again."

Later in the week, in speaking with Michael, Archie's mom was able to understand that her son had seemed angry perhaps because he was feeling guilt about his happiness around his grandfather's death. Michael suggested that now that she had accepted his feelings of anger and relief, Archie would be able to access other feelings, like sadness, underneath.

Sometimes your child may feel anxious as a kind of common denominator of feeling. Once this anxiety is named and tolerated, your child may unearth sadness or anger, or other feelings that have been buried deep down, and can then begin to process them.

Your child may express her feelings as sensations in her body, such as headaches, stomachaches, heaviness, or fatigue. She may find it helpful to know that this is another way her body is telling her how she feels, and you could guide her in identifying the emotion. "I wonder if your stomachache is another way you are feeling your worry?" Although we may not be accustomed to thinking in these ways, we all feel our emotions in our bodies.

A wise elderly relative of Elena's used to say, "Pain shared is pain halved," and this is especially true when speaking to your child about death. When an experience or event is named in a state of togetherness and openness, with a sense of caring, it is much more easily endured. Helping your child find the words for what she is experiencing inside (including feeling numb) is an important step in her gaining a sense of mastery over what may seem overwhelming and bewildering at an already distressing time. At first, you may be uncomfortable saying sentences such as, "I see how hard you are hitting that drum. Maybe you are mad?" But your child will notice when you take the time to work out what she is feeling so that you can lessen her discomfort. Her trust in you will increase, and she will understand the value of expressing her feelings to you. It is an important process and the rewards for you and your child are numerous.

TAKEAWAY

Being numb is a
feeling, too.

The Creative Arts and Your Child's Emotions

We are a highly verbal society and words are a mainstay of how we connect, but it may not always be easy for your child to communicate his internal experience using spoken language. Even though we mean well by it, it is not always helpful when we say to children, "Use your words." As we showed with Renée and her father making art together, there are many different ways of conversing with children as they find their emotional responses to loss. Often as children take in distressing information, they are confronted with events and feelings that are beyond their control and they benefit from having many different tools available for communicating. Creative arts can help adults and children alike to bring their internal experience to the surface in ways that trying to speak about them doesn't, and then it becomes easier to find the words to define the feeling and share it with others. As Renée discovered, drawing is one way that can help to clarify an internal emotional experience.

TAKEAWAY

Art and music can help your child access as well as express his feelings.

Naming Emotions Using the Creative Arts

We have found that these options can be valuable tools:

o   Writing or drawing in a journal or sketchbook

You might find that giving your child different-colored crayons, pencils, and markers encourages her to connect the way she is feeling inside to words or drawings

o   Looking at photographs

Your child might like to see photographs of the deceased person so as to remember and to find her feelings through memories

o   Playing music

You could play music or sing songs that the loved one and your child enjoyed together to help your child recognize how she is feeling

o   Using stuffed animals, dolls, or puppets to start a conversation, with each of you holding one

Parent: "Kitty Cat is feeling sad that Uncle Mort died. She's crying. What does Bunny say?"

o   Reading children's books

> *We list many excellent children's books about emotions in the Resources section*

Seven-year-old Max was struggling to express his emotions after the death of his cousin Damon, who had just started college. Max thought of Damon as a big brother, and when he heard the news he had taken it hard, yelling at his parents, then bolting from the living room to his bedroom. Subsequent efforts by his parents to talk about Damon had been shut down by Max shouting. He had started waking up at night, and at school his teachers said that he seemed combative, which was new and unusual for him. Max's parents weren't sure what to do.

When Max had first met with Elena, he was reluctant to speak with her, and she had given him his own notebook to draw or write something—anything at all. She did this with many of her young patients. For two sessions, Max settled in at a small table and scrawled in the notebook in orange marker until page after page was covered in orange scribble.

"I wonder if that's how you're feeling today, Max?" Elena had asked. "Like the color orange."

Max had shaken his head and continued to scribble.

During their third meeting Elena sat with him quietly, then asked, "If you aren't feeling orange today, is there another color you are feeling?"

Max nodded. "Dark red, but I don't want to feel red so I am drawing orange." He and Elena talked about what made red a color he didn't want to feel.

"Red is yelling and slamming the door," said Max.

"A lot of people use red to show they're feeling mad. I wonder if that is true for you?" asked Elena.

Max nodded.

"Everyone has big mad feelings sometimes. It's part of being a person. We'll think together what to do with all those feelings." Elena paused. "Is there something that is making you mad?"

Max started to talk about Damon. Through his drawing, he had connected his inner experience with the way he was acting, and Elena helped him to understand that he was angry—and that it was okay to feel that way. It was a natural response to the death of someone he had loved very much. She also explained there were things he could learn to do to let those feelings out without getting into fights or yelling.

Finally Max was able to tell his parents, "I'm feeling so mad," making a verbal connection that they could understand and to which they could respond. In contrast, when Max had expressed his emotion by yelling, his parents did not know what he needed. Such behaviors often create barriers to getting help, as parents address what they view as bad behavior instead. In this way, the feelings remain, the child is alone and disconnected, and the parents simmer with frustration.

Now that Max had verbalized how he was feeling, the next step was to find ways to express his anger that weren't hurtful to himself or others. In the next chapter, and in the Resources section, we give ideas for helping your child to manage emotions, including anger, that may appear in the wake of news of a death.

When your child begins to recognize the whole spectrum of feelings that arise within her, she is opening herself up to the full and rich experience of being human, and the more she understands what is going on inside, the more she will realize that other people have emotions, too. As you help your child navigate her emotions, in part by showing her how you feel, you sow the seeds of empathy and create connections between her and others. This will help her as she wrestles with intense emotions after receiving sad news about an illness or death. Her ability to communicate her feelings of grief can make it possible for her to reach out to others who may be experiencing something similar. It doesn't make the feelings go away, but facing them together can be easier. When young Renée watched her father draw a thundercloud of emotions that he felt inside, she was able to understand that he had strong feelings just as she did. That she was not alone. The gray ocean she felt she was drowning in was sadness, a response to her mother's death, and her father was ready to help her swim to shore. Expressing their emotions together would help them through their grief.

Chapter 9

Grief and Mourning: The Immediate Aftermath

✻ Everyone's Grief Is Unique ✻ Dosing of Grief ✻

✻ What Might Grief Look Like ✻ Value in Routines ✻

✻ Methods for Managing Emotions ✻ Mourning Rituals ✻

✻ Attending a Funeral, Burial, or Cremation ✻

✻ Creating Memories ✻ Facing the Reality of Loss ✻

✻ Disenfranchised Grief ✻

G rief is a natural response to the loss of someone or something important, a surge of thoughts and emotions that arise, ebb, and flow over time. Everybody grieves in their own way. While we are primarily focused here on children's feelings of grief after experiencing the death or serious illness of someone close, we acknowledge the importance of grieving other losses, too. These might include the death of a pet, divorce, moving to a new home, or changing schools. The COVID-19 pandemic brought losses large and small into all of our lives and reminded us of the vital role grieving plays in navigating loss of all kinds—and the consequences of not allowing oneself, or being allowed, the time and space to do so. Mourning can be viewed as the external expression of grief and can vary according to culture or religion. It might include rituals such as funerals, memorial services, wearing clothing of specific colors, covering mirrors, or lighting candles or oil lamps, with the aim being to commemorate the person who has died. Our goal in this chapter is to support you in the first days and weeks following the arrival of news of a death in your lives, and to help you understand what grief might look like for your child. We also address questions you may have around your child's participation in mourning rituals.

The Way Children Grieve

Children grieve differently in some ways than adults, and your expectations may not be met. This can be disconcerting at a time when life may already seem chaotic. By being aware of the difference, you can be open to your child's needs and ready to respond even if her behavior may not seem to indicate grief in a way that you readily understand. In our experience, children, more so than adults, often grieve in pockets of time, as they can become overwhelmed by the intensity of their feelings and need to take a break from them. As a reaction, children naturally dose their exposure to their grief by retreating to familiar and comforting activities. They may feel sad and anxious one moment, then leap on a trampoline or giggle with friends the next. This can be confusing to adults, who tend to experience less extreme variations in their feelings and do so with more gradual transitions.

A friend of Michael's son lost his father, a firefighter, on 9/11, and Michael and his young son attended the funeral. The father had been young and well liked and, as with all the 9/11 losses, the shocking and sudden nature of the death brought with it additional sorrow. At the reception following the service, some of the children, Michael's son included, started a riotous game of tag around the tables and chairs, and the grieving son joined in. To some adults, it seemed inappropriate, laughter at a funeral, but it was what the children needed as a release after the intensity of the day. As Michael watched, he felt the heaviness that had settled over him lift for a moment. He looked around the room and saw other adults following the children's antics, too. While some shook their heads, others were smiling. The firefighter's widow stood up, her eyes on her young son as he darted back and forth. She called out his name. For a moment it looked like she might summon him back to his place at the table, accepting condolences from well-wishers, but then she said, "It's okay. You can stay. Go on, play." Michael was struck by the gift she had given her child. He needed to run around and laugh, to dose his grieving. It didn't mean he wasn't still feeling sad and missing his father; he just needed to take a break.

Children often express themselves through play. It can be a way of working out thoughts and is a process through which they gain mastery over situations that are difficult or seem out of their control. Your child is likely to feel unsettled after learning about the death of someone within her world, and she may turn to play as a means of coping. However, even with the knowledge that this is her way of grieving, we understand that it can be unnerving to see your child acting overtly as if a recent death has not affected her in any way. It may be helpful if you can keep the following in mind:

o Everyone's grief is unique

o This may be a new experience for your child and she needs time to process

o Your child needs your support, not your judgment

o Imposing your own feelings will confuse your child rather than make her feel what you feel

o Your disapproval could cause your child to hide her emotions, happy and sad, pushing them away unprocessed

One of Elena's patients, Aaron, came to her for help after his twelve-year-old son died. He was devastated by what he believed to be his young daughter's indifference.

"I thought Sarah loved her brother!" he said. "But all she can do is play with her friends like nothing happened. It's really breaking my heart."

After talking with them both, Elena helped Aaron see that he and his daughter grieved differently, that she missed her brother terribly, but she couldn't stay deep in her sadness the whole time as it was too painful. Though it seemed unimaginable to him, Aaron realized that his daughter needed to go away from the sadness at times and it was good for her to be with her friends.

Over the next few weeks, Aaron told Elena how difficult it was still to hear Sarah's laughter, how it made him tense up inside and feel angry. "I just don't know how she can find anything to laugh about," he said. But he made sure not to reprimand her for her bouts of giddiness, and he let her play with her friends as often as possible. "And we watched a movie together on Saturday," he added. "Sarah cried in parts and wished her brother were watching with us." He paused, choking up. "She really misses him."

The Way Grief May Look in Your Child

In previous chapters we discussed the many different reactions your child might have on learning about a loss, both in the form of questions and through expressing a myriad of different feelings, some completely unexpected. In the days that follow unsettling news, we urge you to continue to validate your child's loss, acknowledge her grief, and let her know that you are keeping a loving eye on her. We encourage you to build on the conversation you started when breaking the news and keep communication going in the days and weeks that follow. It can be helpful to your child if you offer her a road map to grief, telling her she may experience different emotional reactions as the news sinks in and she begins to live with it and process it. Knowing that her feelings are natural responses experienced by many other people can help her see that she is not alone. It can be reassuring to let her know that she will feel better, that one day she will be able to remember the person who died with less sadness, but it can take time.

Grief can manifest as disruptions in your child's behavioral patterns. You may find that your child:

o   Experiences changes in sleep, may have nightmares, and may not want to sleep alone

o   Has struggles around separation

o   Reverts to baby talk, bedwetting, or toileting accidents, or is clingy, constantly whiny, or cranky

o   Is unfocused and distracted

o   Finds school more difficult

o   May not want to be around friends

o   Spends a lot of time watching TV or playing computer games

o   May lack the energy or inclination to do anything at all

o   May have physical symptoms such as a stomachache, headache, lack of appetite, tense muscles, or exhaustion

o   Heads to the school nurse's office more frequently than usual

It can be an especially challenging time for you as a parent, when you may be grieving yourself. But we would say if you can be patient with your child's changes in behavior after a death, and can show as much non-judgmental care and attention as possible at this time, you are likely to help your child's grieving process.

The Value of Keeping to Routines

It is not always easy for parents to know how to treat children in the aftermath of a death or onset of a serious illness. You might wonder if you should go easy on your child for a while to lessen burdens as she navigates grief. We would recommend that you set regular behavioral limits—such as no hitting, while schoolwork, chores, and other responsibilities your child may have should still be done. She should continue to be held accountable for her actions. Your child will feel a sense of security with usual rules and boundaries in place, but we advocate for a softer touch and the understanding that extra love and support, without necessarily talking about the loss, can ease your child's suffering. If your child's behavioral changes continue beyond the first four to six weeks after a loss in a way that interferes with her usual participation in her life, we would recommend that you talk with a professional—her pediatrician, a school counselor, a therapist—to see if she would benefit from more support.

Routines can be beneficial to your child—returning to school or childcare, continuing with hobbies and sports, seeing friends—as they provide structure. This predictability is an antidote to any anxiety he may feel about recent changes in his life. If things feel different within his heart and mind, if his parent(s) seem preoccupied and sad, at least he can know that breakfast is at 7:30 in the morning before school and that teeth get brushed after breakfast and again at bedtime, at 8:30 in the evening. These daily habits are struts, bulwarks against life seeming random and out of control. Try to allow time for talk and hugs, but otherwise it is best for you to model, as far as you are able, that we continue to engage in life and, even though it's not easy, pain is carried.

If your child's loss is of someone with whom he was very close, we would recommend you have him home a little longer, always weighing the benefits of the supportive structure of a daily routine with the comfort of being near you. Much of how you make the decision on when your child should return to activities outside the home will rest on the ability of your child's school or childcare program to be responsive to your child's life change. With a caring environment, being back within the folds of a daily routine is better for your child sooner rather than later.

You may find this list helpful as you prepare for your child's return:

o   Speak, if possible, with his teachers, the school nurse, sport coaches, and other adults who are responsible for his care during the day to inform them of your child's loss.

o   Have conversations about ways in which your child can be best supported and by whom.

o Find ways to help the other children welcome him back in warm but not intrusive ways. (Some children prefer not to have too much attention, as they don't like feeling different from everybody else.)

o Develop a plan in case your child is upset during the day. Can he be offered support through his discomfort by his teacher or the school therapist or counselor rather than being sent home? It's best if he can stay in school through his upset, learning that his school can address his needs.

o Tell your child what the other children know about his situation.

o Give your child language to use in case of questions. "My Gran died. I don't really want to talk about it." Let him know he does not have to get into conversations if he doesn't want to and that he can say something such as, "I really don't feel like talking about it right now."

o The more you can advocate for your child at this time, the smoother the transition back to school is likely to be.

We recognize that many schools are not able to accommodate each child's individual needs, but we believe that if you approach with some ideas and some knowledge about what may be helpful to you and your child, it is easier for teachers and staff to put a plan in place.

Sometimes parents think it is in a child's best interest to keep him home for several weeks after a death, but we believe it is valuable for a child to be back with his peers, resuming the routine of his life, and spending some time away from people who are grieving. Some children are eager to seek out social activity as part of dosing their own grief and your child might let you know that he wants to go back to school. Or he may say he prefers to be at home. While there is no one-size-fits-all guideline, we would say that a return to regular activities would be appropriate for your child when he can concentrate and his emotions are mostly regulated, and his school/childcare can receive him with knowledge, a plan, and care. It is also important to let him know whom to go to for support if he needs it while away from home.

If your child is kept home for weeks on end, it becomes harder for him to return to his previous activities.

One of Michael's patients started to refuse to go to school after the death of her father, not because she was struggling but because she was scared that her mother

> **TAKEAWAY**
>
> A return to regular activities is best when the school/childcare has preparations in place, and your child's emotions are mostly regulated.

would be too sad at home without her. With help from Michael, the mother was able to let her daughter know that she could return to school and her friends. The mother also sought out adult help for herself, inviting her sister to stay with them for a few weeks, so that her daughter would not feel she had to be the caretaker.

When sending your child back to her daily routine beyond the home, let her know that you have spoken with her teachers about what happened and that they will take good care of her. Be aware, though, that even with the best-laid plans, your child may encounter challenges. Her emotions may swing up and down more or she may become preoccupied with body aches and pains. These are signs that she would benefit from more support from you and her teachers and the space to talk about what being back at school is like.

Practicing Self-Care

We know this can be extremely hard on you as a parent and it is important to tend to your own needs as much as possible. This may mean taking time to be by yourself or doing something that restores you. It's helpful to explain to your child that these are ways you manage your feelings and that you will be ready to play or make a snack in a little while. It is a good time to have extra adult hands around if at all possible, though we know it may be likely that can't be arranged. None of this is easy, and we urge you to try to have a healthy diet, to exercise, and get sleep as best you can. These goals may seem nearly impossible as you struggle with your own overwhelming feelings and your child's extra needs, but we believe it is worthwhile for your own well-being—and for your child to see you modeling self-care as part of your own grieving.

TAKEAWAY

Even though there may be much to tend to, take care of your needs with self-compassion.

Methods for Managing Emotions

In the last chapter, we showed you how to help your child to name and express her emotions in order to be able to manage them. Now we would like to share with you ways to teach your child to soothe herself when she finds emotions arising. This ability to manage emotional distress can help her throughout her grieving process but also at any time she is feeling strong or uncomfortable emotions. The important element for her to grasp is that her feelings of grief are natural *and* that she can bear them and get through by understanding them and using tools she can learn. Distress tolerance will stand her in good stead as she undergoes the whirlwind of emotions that often accompany the teenage years. Options for easing challenging emotions include:

o   Listening to music

o Singing songs

o Writing or drawing in a journal, or dictating to someone if unable to write

o Playing a favorite game

o Seeing a friend

o Looking at books

o Engaging with a pet

o Cuddling with a soft toy

o Talking to a loved one on the phone or on a video call

o Cooking or baking with an adult

o Going for a walk

o Breathing exercises (we provide examples in the Resources section)

The activities below can be helpful for all moods but are especially good at allowing your child to release anger or frustration in a productive way:

o Getting moving—dancing, jumping, skipping

o Throwing a soft ball or beanbag at a target

o Pushing on a pillow

o Playing with modeling clay

o Making music with instruments (especially drums)

o Listening to music

o Squeezing squishy toys, even a spongy bat

You might invite your child to join an activity with you: "I'm feeling sad, so I'm putting on this music I like that seems to say just what I feel. Would you like to listen with me?"

If your child is feeling angry, you could make a suggestion such as, "When some people feel mad, they like to bang on a drum." Or, you could create a special place for your child to seek out when she is feeling angry, a "calm-down corner" complete with soothing toys, pillows, and blankets.

As we showed in the last chapter, artwork is wonderfully therapeutic for children. It can help your child as she seeks to give a name to emotions roiling inside, and it may be something that she turns to instinctively to soothe herself as she continues to grieve. You could get out a pile of crayons and paper and say, "I'm going to draw Grandma's garden. She loved spending time there so much." Your child might be tempted to create flowers, too, or something completely different, or she might just observe.

Althea, one of Michael's patients, found it comforting to cook with her young son, Danny, as they both grieved for her mother, his grandmother. Raised in New Orleans, where her mother had lived her entire life, Althea sought solace in cooking red beans and rice, jambalaya, and even cupcakes with purple and green sprinkles for Mardi Gras. As she cooked, Danny measuring and stirring at her side, she told him stories of her childhood, of her mother, and the sharing and memories eased both her pain and his.

The aim as you support your child in his grief is for him to develop the awareness that he can express an emotion and cope with it. He might think, "I know I'm feeling sad and the last time that happened Dad played happy music for me, so I'm going to try that now." Or, "I'm feeling so mad right now that I think I'm going to explode. Gramps taught me to count to twenty and take deep breaths when I feel like this." In this way, he won't feel the need to avoid or ignore emotions and will be able to process his grief fully.

Mourning Rituals

Our society often turns to rituals to mark significant life events—both happy and sad—and we believe in their usefulness in healing for children as well as adults. The kinds of rituals that occur after death depend on the culture and faith of the person who died, but, whatever form they take, we recommend finding ways to include children in the process. Rituals give us all a place and time to express our feelings, often amid other people who are grieving, so they can provide community as well as a way to come to terms with the death.

Should Your Child Attend a Funeral?

One of the first rituals that occurs after a death is the funeral, the details of which will vary depending on a person's belief system.

Often there are events that go along with it—a visitation, a shiva, or a wake, a service, a burial or cremation followed by a social gathering of some kind. Together, these rites can serve several purposes, including celebrating the life of the person who died and, depending on religion, marking the person's entry to the afterlife. In addition, a funeral can acknowledge that someone has died and help to support mourners as they say goodbye together to a person who made an impact on their lives.

TAKEAWAY

If possible, and if you have prepared your child, include him in the rituals following a death.

Parents often ask us whether a child should attend a funeral, and our recommendation is yes, if possible. While you may worry that your child will be overwhelmed by seeing people cry, or expressing grief, it is our view that including children in funerals actually provides the opportunity to process loss and to begin to heal: their feelings are given a concrete place to go and they can be part of a community that is sharing pain. As we saw with virtual funerals during the COVID-19 pandemic, the loss of in-person communal mourning was especially difficult for families and friends to handle. In general, going to a funeral as a family demonstrates that a difficult experience can be made better when it is worked through together. That said, there is planning involved in taking a child to a funeral, and here we guide you through the process to ensure that the experience goes as smoothly as possible.

We recommend that your child attend a funeral with you (whether in-person or virtual), while being aware that each family is different. It is best to describe in as much detail as you can what will happen there to familiarize her with the unfamiliar, as she will find this knowledge calming.

WHY IS THERE A FUNERAL? IT IS:

o   A tradition for family and friends to gather after someone has died

o   A time to say goodbye to the person who has died and to say how much you loved and appreciated them

o   A celebration of their life, a time to remember

o   An occasion to meet up with others who knew the person who died and to mourn together and support one another

o   A time to wish a loved one a good journey to the afterlife, depending on religious beliefs

WHERE WILL THE FUNERAL TAKE PLACE?

o   Will you drive or fly somewhere and stay overnight, or is it close to home?

o Will it take place in a religious setting—a synagogue, church, or mosque? Or at a funeral home? Or crematorium?

o What might the place look like? Big or small? With windows? With rows of chairs?

WHO WILL BE THERE?

o Name specific people: Auntie Jasmine and your cousins; Gran and Gramps

o Name general groups of people: "I think there will be teachers there from the school where Cousin Camilla taught"

o Try to give an indication of how big the crowd will be

WHAT WILL HAPPEN?

o Where will you sit and with whom?

o What will happen at the service? Will there be songs or prayers? Or readings? "Daddy will go to the front and talk about Aunt Renata." "Sometimes we will stand up to sing. We may not know the words to the songs and that is okay. We can just listen."

o Provide some details about the coffin if it will be present, saying that the body of the person who died may be at the front of the room in a kind of box made especially for them and called a coffin, or casket. Often it is covered in beautiful flowers.

o Give details about expected behavior. "Everyone will sit quietly, just like you do during school. If that becomes hard to do, we can go for a little walk, then return."

- o Describe that some people may cry because they are sad. Other people may smile at memories. Others may not show any feelings at all. "You may feel like crying when you're there, or you may not."

- o Explain what people will wear and what clothes your family will wear. "People tend to wear dressing-up clothes, not jeans or shorts." "I'll be wearing my black dress and you'll wear your dark blue pants and sweater."

As always, be open to your child's questions. If she is scared by the idea of attending a funeral, even after your explanation, try to find out what it is that seems challenging rather than assuming it is the funeral itself.

In Chapter 7 you met Theo, who stomped in anger when he learned his grandfather had died. He told his parents he didn't want to attend the funeral. His mother thought he was scared by the idea of the casket, but after gentle questioning it turned out that he had other worries.

"I don't want to sit still for so long," Theo said. "It'll be boring."

His father suggested that he bring along a quiet toy of some kind, and his mother wondered if someone might take him for a walk if he grew restless during the service. With these accommodations in place, Theo felt comfortable enough to go to the funeral with his parents and sister.

He managed to sit quietly through much of it, but when he grew fidgety, his older cousin took him out of the church and for a walk through the grounds.

"We asked him about his experience," his dad told Elena later. "He said the funeral was okay, he was glad to see his cousins, and the cookies at the reception were the best!"

What to Say to a Grieving Person

During mourning rituals you can model for your child what to say to someone whose loved one has died. It is not always easy to find the words and you may feel awkward, but showing that you care is important. Simple phrases such as, "I am so sorry for your loss," "I'm thinking about you and your loved one," or "I just don't know what to say. I'm sorry and I'm here for you," can go a long way. You may worry that saying something will be upsetting to the person who is grieving, but avoiding the subject will be more so. If you find you can't get any words out, then standing quietly by or placing a gentle hand on their arm can express support.

It can be helpful to role-play with your child, if she wants, so that she can experience how it feels to say the words. Ultimately, whether she speaks to the grieving person herself or not, she will take in your condolences, absorb your kindness and compassion, and tuck them away for later.

Should Your Child View an Open Casket?

We are often asked whether children should go to a viewing of the body if there is one, or whether they should look inside an open casket at a funeral. We would suggest that you tell your child what an open casket is, what to expect to see inside, and hear out her reactions. You could say something similar to:

"Grandma's body will be in there and she will be dressed in her favorite red dress. Since she has died, she won't be moving or breathing. She may look different than usual because the funeral workers will put makeup on her face."

You can then decide what you think is best, being sure to tell your child that some people do view and some people don't and it is not about whether one loved the person who died. If your child seems very nervous about it, you would accept those feelings without judgment and see what might help her to be more comfortable. Perhaps she could hold your hand or stand a little bit farther away. If your child still seems very uncomfortable with the idea, we recommend that you say something like, "Let's have you sit with my friend while I go up to the casket and I will come right back and sit with you again." You might explain that going to the casket is another way of saying goodbye but there are many ways to say goodbye and going up to the casket is not necessary unless it feels comfortable.

We do not recommend forcing or pressuring a child to see the body. Equally, if your child has heard an explanation and is at ease with seeing inside the casket, then we propose that you honor her decision—even if it is not something you wish to do yourself.

Should Your Child Attend a Burial?

Some parents worry that a burial may be too upsetting for their child to handle. We suggest a similar approach to the one already offered. Let your child know what will happen at a burial in terms he will understand. You could say something along these lines:

"When the funeral is over, the coffin will be taken to a place called a cemetery or graveyard. There, a deep hole will be dug and the coffin will be lowered into it, then covered up again with dirt. Some people at the burial may pick up a handful of dirt and throw it on top. Sometimes words are said and music may be played."

We encourage you to give your child every opportunity to be present at the burial by answering questions and providing reassurances, but if he is ultimately too upset about it, we feel it is less important to attend than the funeral itself.

Talking About Cremation

Some families choose cremation rather than a traditional burial, and a memorial service might take place at a crematorium. To help your child understand what happens during cremation, we suggest language such as, "The body is turned into ashes by fire and the ashes are put into a special container that can be kept. Some people scatter the ashes later in places that the loved one enjoyed."

✻ ✻ ✻

If you feel that your child can't be comfortably prepared, despite your best efforts, and so won't attend a funeral service, don't make him feel excluded. Try to find other ways to involve him in remembering and paying tribute to your loved one. He could make a card or write a statement of love that someone else could read at the funeral. This would be helpful to him, to give his feelings a place to go and to know that he still participated. Tell your child about the service when you return to give him a sense of what it was like. Sometimes families choose to have funerals filmed, and this could be a way for your child to see the service without the intensity of being there. It would also be available for your child to view as he matures and per¹.aps decides a few years later that he would like to see what happened.

Creating Memories

There may be other private rituals surrounding a death, and we encourage you to find ways to let your child participate. It could be planting a tree together in the name of the person who died or gathering with cousins to sing a song your loved one enjoyed. Getting together with other family members over a meal is a wonderful and meaningful way to share stories and is accessible to even the youngest child.

When the Reality of Death Sets In

Many young children need time to understand the implications of death, to see what finality means in their lives. They may not be able to take it in until the funeral occurs, or their teacher does not return to school after winter break, or Uncle Nat doesn't carve the turkey at Thanksgiving dinner. A child who has been told his father has died might ask when Dad is coming home many times over as a way of trying to process the news that his father is no longer around. This "goneness" can take some time to accept and your child will need your support.

A funeral can mark the end of the flurry of activity around a death and can be the time when a child may begin to come to terms with how her life has changed. If the loved one who died was a central part of your child's life, there may be considerable emotional and practical challenges to face. Some children may have to find ways to adapt as they return to the new realities of day-to-day life and to potential variations in their customary routines. These secondary losses could mean big changes in the future if the death has affected the family's financial status. There could be a move to a new home or a change in school. Something as seemingly innocuous as a school event such as "Grandparents Day" can cause a child to question her identity—am I still a granddaughter? This can be a time when sitting with a child and being able to talk about difficult subjects is especially important. Your child will appreciate your honesty, your time spent with her, and the care you show. In Chapter 14, we look in more depth at the ways in which grief is processed over time.

Disenfranchised Grief

We believe it is important to recognize and provide space for grief after losses of all kinds. Disenfranchised grief, or hidden grief, is the name given to loss that is not openly acknowledged, publicly mourned, or socially supported. It is often discounted or misunderstood by others, which makes it challenging to process, leaving it to fester.

This kind of grief may affect your child in several ways:

Miscarriage or Stillbirth

Disenfranchised grief can occur after a miscarriage or stillbirth, as friends and family could minimize the death and may have little understanding about the emotional pain felt by parents at the time of loss and long afterward. If the pregnancy had not been made public, there may be the additional burden of grieving alone. If you (or someone within your child's world) are grieving a miscarriage, you may find it difficult to express your emotions without a social support system to do so or you may bear the brunt of others' unintentionally hurtful comments. We encourage you to allow yourself to grieve and to express your needs to others. In Chapter 13 we go into more depth on speaking to your child about these difficult and painful situations.

Unrecognized Relationships

One of Elena's patients, a nine-year-old named Momo, struggled to express her grief when her stepmother died. Momo hadn't been close to her, as her father and his new wife lived on the other side of the country, but she had liked her and was sorry that she had died. However, Momo knew that her mother was still angry about her father remarrying and so she was scared to show her grief in case she upset her. She started having stomachaches and waking in the night. She was struggling with disenfranchised grief. In speaking with Momo and her mother, Elena helped them to see that Momo's grief needed to be acknowledged. The mother found it hard to accept that her daughter could have feelings for her stepmother, as it felt like a betrayal, but eventually she was able to validate Momo's loss and give her permission to grieve. Elena helped her to find ways to be with Momo in her grief, and the mother began to feel less upset by her daughter's attachment to her stepmother.

These feelings of unacknowledged grief can occur in multiple ways as family structures shift and blend, as people children have grown attached to die or disappear from their lives for other reasons, such as divorce, relationship breakups, moving house, life changes, etc.

Death of a Pet

Sometimes parents don't give appropriate attention to a child's grief about the death of a pet. They might suggest they can just buy another one. Maybe that is the case—and maybe they will—but the child's loss and her grief must be acknowledged first. Only once that is done can the child begin to handle the emotions around the loss. It can be helpful to have a small tribute to the pet that died. You could gather the family around a photo of the pet and each person could share a memory, or what they liked about him, and say goodbye. We offer support and advice on pets and euthanasia in Chapter 10.

Less-Significant Loss

Not all loss involves the loss of life, but it may still feel significant to your child. The pandemic brought with it losses large and small, and while many people grieved the deaths of loved ones who died from COVID, many others did not grieve for losses that felt insubstantial in comparison. Perhaps the loss of a vacation, or time with grand-children, a missed middle-school graduation, or a child's first day of kindergarten.

Children may have feelings of grief after losing a favorite toy or moving to a new home or during a divorce. Expressing these emotions is natural and our advice is to acknowledge that the grief is real. In this way, it can be dealt with. Help your child to write a letter to her lost stuffed cat, so that she can tell him in an imaginary way that she hopes he's okay and that she's missing him. Perhaps create a scrapbook of happy memories and photographs of the old home with your child. Let your child know that it is okay to be upset about your divorce and come up with ways to help him to process. Validate feelings of grief. There is no rating system for what should or should not be grieved for.

Disproportionate Grief

Sometimes the grief your child expresses over a death may seem disproportionate and so might be dismissed. Perhaps your child is distraught when you tell her about the death of an uncle that she rarely saw. You might want to respond to her flood of tears with, "But you barely knew him!" Instead, it is best to acknowledge her reaction and show support. Her feelings may include grief about past losses.

We know that it can be extremely hard to see your child suffer as he grieves, especially as you may be struggling with your own feelings around the loss. It may be difficult to see beyond the current moment, but we would like to let you know that your child can come through it with your help, the support of friends, family, and community, and your courageous conversations. Facing his grief will empower him to face other difficult situations and emotions that may lie ahead. From out of this pain can come growth, grit, and greater compassion.

Chapter 10

When a Loved One Has a Terminal Illness

❋ Facing the Unthinkable ❋ Breaking the News ❋
❋ Anticipatory Grief ❋ Making Amends ❋ Reframing Expectations ❋
❋ Enjoying the Moment ❋ Redefining Hope ❋ Arranging a Visit ❋
❋ Saying Goodbye ❋ When a Pet Is Terminally Ill ❋

The idea of telling a child that a family member or someone else important to her is going to die is a daunting prospect, and one that many parents might choose to avoid. We are often asked, "Do we really need to say he's going to die? Can't we wait until after it's happened?" Parents may hold a well-intentioned belief that their child does not need to know that a loved one has a terminal illness and that telling her will cause her unnecessary sadness that she will inevitably have to experience all over again after the death. This is a common parent pitfall. While it is understandable that you might withhold the facts, it is not in your child's best interest. In this situation we recommend that you tell your child the truth as soon as you are emotionally able. Our reasons for doing so include: your child is likely to find out about a terminal illness whether you tell her or not and may develop her own (potentially more distressing) narratives; a child who knows a loved one will die can begin to prepare emotionally for the death while enjoying precious remaining time with the person, which will help her to cope after the death; an anticipated death gives her the opportunity to say goodbye; and involving her in such a hard conversation helps her to know she is included in important happenings in your family. In this chapter, we will help you to understand the reasons for letting your child know, and provide you with the tools to have the conversation and to support your child as she processes the news.

TAKEAWAY

It is best to tell your child the truth about a loved one's confirmed terminal illness as soon as you are emotionally able.

Michael met with five-year-old Catalina after several weeks of her having tantrums before school and bad dreams that wakened her nightly. During the session, he asked if something was upsetting her. Catalina paused, her face serious, then said, "Mommy is going to die. Daddy was crying and talking to Aunt Gabi on the phone." In speaking with Catalina's parents, Michael discovered that the young girl had misunderstood. It was her grandmother who had a terminal illness. Now that her parents knew the reason for Catalina's upset, they were able to tell her the truth and support her as she took in the news.

Once you, as a parent, learn that someone in your child's world has been diagnosed with a terminal illness, it is likely that your child will sense something is going on. It may be that your demeanor has changed—you may be preoccupied or sad—or that your child has overheard whispered conversations among adults. Whatever it is, it is our experience that your child will inevitably intuit that things have shifted within his world, although he may not have the words to name what exactly, or to form questions that might prompt explanation and connection. Young children can become confused when their knowledge is limited and may come to incorrect conclusions. In the face of withheld information they are often left alone with overwhelming feelings of anxiety and fear. Sometimes, as with Catalina, their imaginings based on incomplete knowledge may be even worse than the truth you are trying to shield them from. Very often when children sense that something is not quite right in their world, their thoughts will turn to something being very wrong with their parents. Instead, when you give your child clear and simple information and the space to ask questions, his anxiety diminishes because he is validated in his sense that something was off, and he can face the reality—whatever it is—with you, knowing he has your support and that the loved one is being cared for.

Breaking the News of Terminal Illness

First, we think it is helpful to clarify what we mean by terminal illness, as many parents have asked us at what stage of an illness is it appropriate to tell a child. If someone important to your child receives news of a life-threatening (but not terminal) illness, we think it is a good idea to let your child know: "Cousin Rob's doctors told him today that he has a big sickness—his heart is not working very well. He's going to take some time off work to rest while the medicines work."

If the doctors believe there is a chance of a cure, then we would recommend you don't talk about death. If your child says, "Will he die?" you might respond:

"The doctors are using strong medicines and are hopeful that he will recover."

Only when doctors have said there is no hope of cure for a disease and that death is likely within a few months (or less) would we say that this is terminal illness. However, each situation is unique and we are aware that this may be hard to gauge. You may have to navigate other people's needs, comfort level, and emotions as well as your own. There may be different stages in the illness even once you know it is terminal. However, keep in mind the importance of not losing your child's trust, and when the emotional tenor has changed in your household, we suggest you have another conversation with your child that reflects the new reality.

If the medicines do not seem to be working but death is not imminent, you might say that the illness has progressed and that the person is much sicker. If your child asks if death is a possibility, you can confirm that. Giving children incremental information—as long as you are being truthful—can help them to absorb and process the news more easily.

For breaking the news that a person's illness is terminal and that death is likely soon, we propose that you do so in the same way as telling your child about a death. First try to take the time to know your own feelings about how ill the person is so that you can ground yourself and prepare emotionally to address your child's needs in your conversation. When you are ready—and as quickly as you are able—choose a place that enables you to be private and comfortable as a family, and a time that allows for you all to be together for a while afterward.

> **TAKEAWAY**
>
> Plan for the conversation to take place in a quiet area, not right before bedtime, and when there is plenty of time for talk and being together after.

We suggest using language such as:

"We have some very sad news to share together. The doctors told us that Aunt Shonda has a big sickness and they have no more medicines to make her better."

Or, "We have some very sad news and we're going to spend some time together. As you know, Aunt Shonda is ill. Her doctors have said that her sickness is too big for the medicines to work anymore."

After a pause to allow your words to sink in and for any immediate reactions to emerge, you could add: "Aunt Shonda is going to die. We don't know exactly when, but sometime after school is over." It can help your child to have the timing linked to a known event in his life or to a season so that he has something solid to hold on to.

If no questions or comments arise, you could say, "This is a lot for you to take in. How is it for you?"

This may be followed by a stymied silence, so you might continue:

"It's hard to know sometimes. I have a lot of feelings right now and you may be feeling lots of different ways, too."

If your child doesn't have any response now, it probably signals that this may be enough for this initial conversation. Since anxiety can make new information hard to handle (especially when it is upsetting), be sure to communicate that you are open to questions whenever they arise and that there will be other opportunities to continue talking.

If the person who is terminally ill is close to your child,
it is also important to let your
child know that you will tell
his teachers so that he can
get help when he is away from
home if he is feeling upset or
wants to talk.

TAKEAWAY

This conversation is a
process that takes place
over time, as concerns,
questions, and new
information arise.

Common Questions

Over the years, we have found that several common questions come
up during the initial conversation or later, and we share answers
here that you may find helpful:

Why Can't the Doctor Make Him Better?

This query taps into what we all wish we could believe: that doctors
know how to cure every illness. It is possible to convey belief in
doctors, an important basic safety your child needs, and also to
acknowledge the reality that doctors don't always have all the
answers. A possible answer might be along the lines of:

"His doctors have kept him well for as long as they can, but they
don't have the medicines yet to make this sickness better. One day
we hope that doctors will have all the medicines they need
to fix the sickness that he has."

Can't We Do Something to Make Her Better? What If My Sister and I Stop Fighting? What If We Get Her a Puppy?

Young children often think that by wishing for something strongly
enough they can make it happen. It's hard to accept that something
important can't be fixed and something bad is going to occur. A
possible answer may be:

"We all wish that there is something we could do to make her sickness go away. We can try to make her feel better, but we can't make her live longer. Knowing how much we love her helps her feel less sad, and we can think of ways to show her that we are thinking of her."

When Is He Going to Die?

Children find uncertainty difficult to handle. It's uncomfortable not to know when something big is going to happen. This is a challenge, and acknowledging this to your child helps. An answer could be:

"No one is sure exactly when he will die. That is not something that can be known. It's so hard not to know when, but we will tell you when we have more information and definitely when it happens."

Where Will She Be When She Dies?

Young children are very literal. Knowing details such as a location helps to anchor their understanding. An answer may be:

"She will probably be in bed in the hospital or at home. That's another one of those things we can't know for sure."

As you speak with your child, it can be helpful to convey that by being together and supportive of one another, you will all be able to get through this difficult time. You might say, "We are so sad about the news and it's hard to imagine feeling better, but we are all here and we will make it through." You would also provide hope for the person who is dying by identifying what she may still be able to do. "The doctors are doing a lot to help Aunt Shonda feel comfortable. She is still watching some of her favorite TV shows, and I gave her some pictures of you that make her smile."

We know that none of this is easy, but we do believe that a certain amount of peace and understanding will come about after having multiple conversations with your child about an impending death, and that having these conversations prior to the death can mean that everyone will have an easier time handling the loss when it happens. In our experience, we have seen that once children learn that a loved one will die, they begin to internally process the news in a way that helps to prepare them for the eventual death. This is called anticipatory grief. It does not take away the sadness and shock (and/or all the other emotions) they may feel—and will feel again when the person dies—but it does bring with it a sense of preparedness.

Sometimes young children are astonished after a loved one has died that the world can go on. This highlights that the best time to intervene and reassure children is before a death. It is helpful to let your child know that the family will continue to cope after the person has died, and that she will continue to be loved and cared for. You would hope to convey in your conversations that what is happening is upsetting and that you will get to the other side together. "It's very sad that Grandpa will die soon, and we won't be able to spend time with him as usual in the summer. But we will get through this together. We'll make other plans for the summer and we'll have happy memories of Grandpa."

Uncle Jamar was seven-year-old Joya's favorite relative and she loved him coming over for dinner every Sunday. A couple of years earlier, Jamar was diagnosed with lung cancer and Joya was told he had a big sickness and was getting good care and medicines from his doctors. However, now the cancer had spread, and Jamar had only a matter of weeks to live. His brother, Ray, and sister-in-law Darlene were devastated. They had no idea what to tell Joya, though they felt in their hearts they had to say something. They met with Elena for a consultation.

After listening to their concerns and exploring their feelings about Jamar being terminally ill, Elena helped them with language to let

Joya know what was going on, saying it was likely that she already knew a little, even if she wasn't showing any behavioral changes or asking questions.

The next day, Ray and Darlene sat down with their young daughter and told her that Uncle Jamar's big sickness had become much worse and that the medicines the doctors were using could not make him better. They said that he was going to die.

Joya looked at them and then yelled, "No!" Darlene and Ray began to cry and Joya started to sob.

"I want to see him!" said Joya. "I don't want him to die." She paused. "Was that why you were crying yesterday, Daddy?"

Ray told Elena the next week, "At that moment, painful though it was, I knew we had done the right thing. Because she can still see Jamar. For now."

"I can't imagine what she would have done if we had just told her he had died," said Darlene.

"You did something very difficult," said Elena. "It may not seem like it now but you have given Joya a gift."

Processing the News

When you tell your child that a loved one will die soon, he is able to continue his relationship with the person in the knowledge that the person will not be alive much longer. Sometimes when someone dies unexpectedly, people—adults and children alike—can be left with feelings of guilt about things said or not said, done or not done. Knowledge of a death ahead of time will not erase such feelings, but it may mean that regrets can be addressed before it is too late.

If your child says something unkind about someone who is dying, "I don't want to see Cousin Mimi. She smells weird!," there is still the opportunity to talk through what he has said. Without the knowledge of an impending death, those words or others like them may not be amended and your child could be left feeling guilty.

Even as your child grapples with the idea of letting go, it can be helpful if you can guide him to find joy in the here and now. Instead of focusing on how upsetting it will be when your loved one dies, strive to be aware of each day or each hour you get to spend with her, and to model that for your child. As humans, it is our nature to try to feel less attached to someone before they die, to lessen the pain, so try to be alert to this and to enjoy the time you have.

If your child is frustrated by changes in the person she loves, try to be patient. "Why can't Gran come for my birthday this year? No fair! She always does." It can be hard to remain calm and remind your child that Gran's sickness is stopping her from making the journey this year. "We're mad at Gran's big illness, too, and wish she could visit, but this year we are visiting her instead. We think it will be a lot of fun."

> **TAKEAWAY**
>
> Encourage your child to make the most of the time remaining with the person who is dying.

Remember that your child's behavior may seem out of sync with the situation but that is because she is learning. This is an opportunity for you to teach your child and to model compassion.

Encourage your child to reframe the situation and think about things she can still enjoy with her loved one, rather than getting mired in the things she cannot. "Would you like to think of something you can do with Gran?" You might inspire your child to brainstorm.

You can also talk to your child about redefining hope for her loved one as an illness progresses. Instead of hoping for a longer life for the person who is dying, she could wish her the most comfort and enjoyment possible in the remaining time. Perhaps from "I hope Mrs. Gaskill can come to our songfest," to "I hope Mrs. Gaskill can listen to the songs we sang and sent to her," to "I hope Mrs. Gaskill isn't suffering."

With guidance from Elena, Darlene and Ray were able to support Joya as she continued her relationship with Uncle Jamar. He came home from the hospital, and palliative-care doctors and nurses took care of him, managing his pain. He was too tired to visit on Sundays and, while this was disappointing to Joya, she started to speak with him by phone during dinner so they could be together still. She enjoyed hearing his voice and telling him about her week, and when speaking became too exhausting for him, she sang songs to him instead.

While distressing, the time leading up to death need not be filled with sorrow. During her own daughter's terminal illness, Elena remembers a friend visiting who told her later that she had expected the whole household to be crushed with sadness and gloom. Instead, the friend had arrived to find folk songs playing, Elena baking chocolate chip cookies in the kitchen, and her daughters lying on the couch, enrapt in a favorite movie. The visit passed with laughter and conversation, and the friend still cherishes the memory of the afternoon spent together. With little time left with someone with a terminal illness, you can assist your child to make the most of what remains.

When children are not told beforehand about a death, they often say later that they wish they could have said goodbye, or made amends, or told the person, "I love you."

Should My Child Visit?

Many parents have asked us whether their child should visit someone who is terminally ill, and we recommend that children be given the opportunity to do so. Young children do better with new

---

TAKEAWAY
Being able to be with the person dying allows your child to build memories with them.

---

experiences in general when they have an idea of what to expect, whether it's a visit to the dentist or their first day of school. We advise you to tell your child as many details as possible about what a visit with a terminally ill person might entail.

o   When would the visit take place?

o   Where will it be?

> *At home or a hospital?*

> *What will the person's room look like?*

> *Will there be medical equipment there?*

o   What will the sick person look like?

> *Will they be in bed?*

> *Will their appearance have changed, and how?*

> *Will they have medical tubes?*

> *Will they be awake?*

> *Will they be able to speak?*

> *Will they recognize the child?*

o   Who will be there?

> *Will doctors and nurses be present?*

> *Will other visitors be there?*

o   What will happen?

> *Sitting with the sick person*

> *Conversations with other visitors*

o How long will the visit last?

Is there an opportunity to leave after a short while?

o What might the child do?

Bring a toy or coloring books

Read books

Play on an electronic device

If your child seems reluctant about a visit, we do not recommend forcing one. Instead, we suggest exploring what it is about the visit that might be making your child hesitant and then offering to help her with it. If your child is still convinced that she prefers not to visit, we advise that you help her to express her love for the sick person in another way. Perhaps by making a card, writing a note, or drawing a picture.

One of Michael's patients took his children to visit their grandfather who was dying of heart disease. He and his wife had explained everything that the children might encounter ahead of time.

On arrival, their grandfather was sleeping and the children sat quietly. The minutes passed and still Grandpa slept. Maya brought out a puzzle and put it on the end of the bed. "Want to play, Grandpa?" she asked.

"He's sleeping," said Jonah. "He can't play a puzzle. That's dumb."

He reached for the puzzle and pushed it off the bed and onto the floor, where it landed with a clatter.

"Mom!" shouted Maya. Then she burst into tears.

"I don't want to be here," said Jonah. "This is boring."

Even with the best preparation, sometimes things don't go according to plan and you may have to adjust. It can be helpful to use the best practice *Expect the unexpected.* In this case, the children were taken downstairs and into the yard, where they played and waited for their father.

When Michael discussed the visit with his patient, he wondered if Jonah had behaved as he did because the visit had made his grandfather's impending death more real for him, and it was hard for him to take it in. He recommended a gentle conversation with Jonah that week to acknowledge the boy's concern, to talk about how different his grandfather's illness had made him, and to plan for the next visit. "You could say it's a chance for him to let his grandpa know that he cares about him," suggested Michael.

The next Sunday, another visit took place and it went much better. Maya and Jonah had already seen their sick grandfather sleeping and had talked about it with their parents. This time they sat at his bedside for a little while, told him they loved him, and left cards before heading back downstairs.

Saying Goodbye

We believe it is in a child's best interest to have the opportunity to bid farewell to a loved one, when possible. This can soften the impact of the loss when it occurs, as it can be a concrete positive moment for children to hold on to as they grieve. We have seen the way that granting last wishes is healing for those who are terminally ill and for their loved ones, as it provides a sense of purpose in final days, gives feelings a place to go, and ensures that the person who is dying feels honored. These wishes can be as simple as bringing flowers, sharing a favorite bite of food, or watching a funny movie together.

When doctors said that Uncle Jamar would die within a few days, Ray and Darlene asked Joya if she would like to visit to say goodbye. Elena had suggested it would be a good idea, if possible. At first, Joya was scared at the prospect.

"What if he looks weird?"

"Well," said her mom. "He is thin. You've seen that on video calls. He'll be in bed, probably sleeping. There'll be a nurse there to look after him and he has a plastic tube in his arm for the medicine to go in."

"Let's think on it," said her dad. "You don't have to go, but know we will be there, and if you feel uncomfortable, we can leave."

Later Joya told her parents that she wanted to visit and the next day they went to her uncle's house. He lay in his bed with his eyes closed, but when the nurse said, "Joya is here for you, Jamar," he smiled and his eyes flickered open. They sat with Uncle Jamar for a little while and when it was time to leave, Joya leaned close to him. "Goodbye, Uncle Jamar," she said. "I love you so much." She felt him gently squeeze her hand.

A couple of days later, Joya learned that her uncle had died and she sobbed and sobbed. Though she knew that it would happen, it still hurt very much. After his death, Elena continued to talk to Ray and Darlene about how they were all doing. Both parents felt relieved that they hadn't surprised Joya with the news of Jamar's death and that they had laid the groundwork for coping with it together. Joya felt comfortable talking about her uncle and had good memories of him. This helped Ray enormously as he processed the loss of his brother.

Growing Resilience

As Joya grows older, she is likely to recognize that her parents had some very difficult conversations with her about Jamar's illness and death and included her in an important process. This will lead to a deepening bond and increased trust. In addition, she may feel a sense of pride in the way they confronted something painful head-on and will realize that she too faced a challenging situation and, with their guidance, was able to navigate to the other side. Working through a problem—no matter how distressing—instead of avoiding it increases a child's self-esteem and sense of mastery over difficult things. Joya will be able to say, "I've done this before.

It's hard but I know I can do it again." It's a way of developing resilience and grit.

We know how difficult these conversations about terminal illness can be for parents. We have also seen the many ways in which they may provide you with relief. Being honest means that you can be your authentic self, and not worry about hiding important information from your child—while still being selective in which details to share. You and your child are both in the experience together, and trying to create good memories of the dying person for your child may help you stay in the here and now. To take in and enjoy the person in the moment. There is strength and purpose in that.

When a Pet Has a Terminal Illness

For many households, a pet is viewed as a member of the family and when a veterinarian diagnoses a terminal illness, the news can be hard to bear. It can be especially heartbreaking to tell your children. Many parents have asked us for help in finding language to convey this upsetting news and for advice on supporting their children through the illness, the decision to end the pet's life (if necessary), the death, and its aftermath.

Our advice is to tell your child about your pet's illness when you know instead of waiting until after the death. We offer some specific advice here to help you through this difficult time.

Preparing to Tell Your Child

Know Your Own Thoughts and Feelings

We recommend that you take a little time to sit with the news yourself and to understand the emotions stirring inside. Many people have close bonds with their pets and you may be shaken and upset. You may have had your pet for many years, passed through major and minor life events with him at your side, so allow yourself to feel these emotions. If there's a voice inside chastising you for being upset about "just a dog" or "just a cat," allow yourself to validate your thoughts about the impending loss and to acknowledge the grief you feel. Be aware that news of the terminal illness may bring on thoughts of other illnesses you may have dealt with, or other deaths, of pets or humans.

Understanding the degree and complexity of emotions inside you will help you to gain a little distance from them and to stabilize yourself. Once you have readied yourself in this way, you will be better able to take care of your child's needs and reactions when you speak with him.

Know Your Child

While you won't be able to predict your child's exact reaction to the news, it can be helpful to have some idea of how she might respond and how best to support her. You could ask yourself the following questions:

o How will the death of the pet affect your child's life?

   Does she help with the pet's care? Feeding, walking, grooming?

   Does she play with the pet? How often?

   Does she turn to the pet at certain times for comfort?

o What is your child's experience with death in her life?

   Does she understand what death means?

o How has your child reacted to loss, separation, or death in the past?

o How does your child like to be helped when she experiences strong emotions?

   Does she like to be held or hugged?

   Does she like to be given space?

Breaking the News

When you are ready to give your child the news, choose a time and a private place where you can be together for a while. It's best to give the information as a family, if possible, and it can be helpful to have another adult present. You might like to have the pet there if you can. We recommend that you keep your language simple and age-appropriate and steer clear of euphemisms for death. You might say some version of this:

"We have some sad news to tell you. We heard from the vet today that Dodger has a sickness called cancer and that the vet's medicine can't fix him. He is going to die. Let's all have some time with each other now."

Sit with your child as she responds to the news with questions and/or emotions, answering honestly with as much information as you can give. She is likely to want to know why and when your pet will die. She may worry that she has caused the illness. You can let her know that nothing she did or said (or omitted to do or say) could have caused this illness in any way.

She may ask if your pet is in pain, and you could give her a truthful answer. You would say no if he is not, and if he is, you could say something such as, "He is in some pain, but I am giving him medicine from the vet and that is making the pain better."

Your vet may have recommended euthanasia to end the suffering, and if this is the case, we suggest that you let your child know this as a second step in breaking the news. First, let your child take in the details of the pet's illness and absorb the fact that he will die, and then revisit the conversation later while adding the new information. When exactly you address the second part will depend on the severity of your pet's illness and when the euthanasia will take place.

We advise you to say something such as, "You know how we told you that Dodger is sick, and there aren't any medicines to make him better? His illness hurts him sometimes and because we love him we don't want him to suffer anymore. The veterinarian is going to come here and give him a strong drug that's just for animals that will help him to die in peace. This is something that animal doctors do for many pets when they are suffering and can't get better."

While the process of euthanasia is often referred to as "putting to sleep," we strongly advise against calling it that. It will not ease your child's pain but may instead cause her confusion and possibly fear around going to sleep herself. Some people like to evoke happy images for their children of the big dog park in the sky or something similar, depending on the pet. We believe it is fine to use such imagery as long as your child understands that the death of the pet will be permanent, that the pet will not be able to do any of the things he did while alive, that the death is happening because the pet's body is not working anymore, and that it is not possible to visit the pet.

As your child takes in the news, she is likely to want to know when this will happen. If it is feasible, and your pet is not in too much pain, it can be helpful to have a day to prepare to say goodbye.

Your child may ask immediately if she can get a new pet. While it could be distressing to hear this question, try to accept it as your child's way of processing the information. Perhaps it is a way of saying she'll miss her pet so much that she wants something to make her feel the pet's absence less. It does not mean that she is callous or thoughtless—she is a young child grappling with something upsetting and possibly completely new to her. We recommend you respond gently, saying something along the lines of:

"I know how much you love Dodger, and how much you love dogs. Let's talk about another dog when school is finished for the year."

Some children may be curious about the pet's illness or the process of euthanasia, and we would encourage you to answers questions truthfully while only providing information appropriate to her level of understanding.

Saying Goodbye

Some families say goodbye to their pet by making sure she gets all her favorite things on her final day: a long nap in a sunny patch, some catnip, a much-loved food or treat, a short walk and sniff in the yard. If you decide to do something like this, while it may be difficult, try to enjoy the present moment, modeling for your child the importance of celebrating the time you have left with your pet and the memories you are making. Try to give everyone in the family an opportunity to tell the pet how much she means to each of you and to reminisce.

Should My Child Be Present at the Euthanasia?

Not all veterinarians are comfortable with young children attending a euthanasia process, so it is best to find out and, if necessary, to find one who supports family-present euthanasia. You may also want to discuss whether a home-based euthanasia is best for your family and if that is possible.

In general, we recommend that you give your child the opportunity to be present so she is not left alone to wonder about the process and potentially come up with her own alternative and possibly frightening narrative. We believe in sending the message that the family can get through this upsetting process together, by supporting one another. We recommend that you prepare for the euthanasia by finding out what will happen and sharing the details with your child so that she can know what to expect. With this knowledge, she can make a decision on whether to attend. If she seems reluctant, try to find out why and see if you can make accommodations. It may be helpful to have another adult present who can take your child for a walk if she changes her mind at the last minute or becomes upset or bored. Whether your child attends or not, make sure she has a chance to say goodbye. You could take a snippet of your pet's fur (or a feather) or make a mold of his paw in clay to commemorate him.

Your child may want to know what happens to the pet's body after death and your veterinarian can be helpful here. Options may include burial in a place of your or the vet's choosing, or cremation—with ashes returned to the family. In the latter case, you might choose to scatter ashes with your child in a place that your pet loved.

Remembering Your Pet

It is helpful for your child's grief process if you provide ways to memorialize your pet. You could plant flowers or a tree in your yard with a plaque commemorating your pet's life. Your child could paint pictures or write a story or a poem about the pet, or together you could create a photo album or slideshow of your favorite memories. Your child might like to keep a pet's favorite toy. There are many options, no right or wrong, and you can choose what would work best for you and your child. The idea is to show your child that memories continue even after death, that it is okay to talk about a pet that has died, and that in doing so she is continuing to express her love for her pet.

Chapter 11

Talking to Your Child About a Death by Suicide

✳ Why to Tell ✳ Breaking the News About the Suicide of
Someone Close ✳ Language Around Suicide ✳
✳ Answering "Why Did It Happen?" ✳ Suicide as a Disease ✳
✳ Teaching Compassion ✳ There Is Always Hope ✳
✳ Suicide in the Community ✳ Suicide in the Media ✳
✳ Meeting Your Child Where She Is ✳ Communication Is Key ✳
✳ Planting Seeds for Lifesaving Conversations ✳

Every fiber of your being as a parent may want to resist the idea of talking about suicide with your child, and we understand that. It's a very difficult subject to discuss, even for adults. You may think, "My child is too young. She couldn't possibly understand," or "It's too scary a subject. There's no reason he needs to know about it." There may be elements of truth in these thoughts and our recommendation is to not bring up the topic until it is necessary. However, we believe it is in your best interest to have some idea of how to talk about suicide with your young child for when the need arises. In our experience, there are two distinct situations in which you may have to navigate this conversation: if someone important to you and your child dies by suicide and when suicide touches your child's life in a more distant way. Our aim in this chapter is to help you understand why it is beneficial for your child to have your guidance around suicide, to provide you with language to speak to him about this uncomfortable subject, and to build the groundwork for potentially lifesaving conversations as he grows into a teenager and young adult.

> **TAKEAWAY**
> It is likely your child will hear about suicide during her childhood—and it is best to be ready to talk about it with her.

When Someone Close to You Dies by Suicide

When suicide is the cause of death of someone in or close to your family, then our recommendation is to tell the truth to your child if he is around the age of six or older. We believe that children younger than six could be told that someone has died and then later, when they are older and are more able to handle the information, the conversation would be revisited and they can be given more details. Our reasoning for these recommendations is multifold:

- In our experience, we have found that from this age children have the capacity to understand what suicide means.

- Your school-age child spends time around people other than his parents and may have access to the Internet and so is likely to find out the truth from others in a direct or indirect way. Children are adept at rooting out information and can often find themselves alone with confusing details. This can be especially troubling around a suicide.

- If your child discovers at the time or later that you have hidden knowledge from him, he may feel betrayed by your apparent lack of trust and could doubt your words in the future.

- At funerals, suicide as the cause of death may be stated, and your child's sudden discovery of the truth at an already overwhelming time could make it hard for him to manage his emotions—including anger toward you.

- When your child gleans details about a death from other people's stories and conversations, you lose control of the delivery of information. He may hear distortions and judgments as he absorbs the news elsewhere.

- When you break the news to your child at a time of your choosing, you can support him as he processes the information in the moment and as questions arise in the days that follow.

- Speaking with your child about the suicide of someone important to him creates and strengthens trust, sends the message that you are open to talking about difficult subjects, and facilitates future conversations.

- A family history of suicide is considered a risk factor for suicide in a related family member and awareness of this could be lifesaving in the future.

One of Michael's patients, Rana, an eleven-year-old girl, was furious with her parents when she learned that her older cousin had died by suicide. He had died when she was eight, in a car accident she was told, and her parents had not allowed her to attend his funeral. Recently Rana's uncle had mentioned something in passing and she realized the truth. Confused and upset by the news, Rana didn't know what to think, or whom to turn to for answers. She felt she couldn't trust her parents to be honest. Her emotions tangled inside her—frustration with her parents, anger at her cousin, shame for feeling that way, confusion about why he had taken his own life, sorrow about the death all over again. Eventually, Rana's parents took her to see Michael so that she could process her cousin's death, and they could find a way to rebuild their own relationship with her.

Breaking the News

Breaking the news to your child about a death by suicide is difficult and we hope to offer you structure and a path forward as a way to keep you grounded as much as possible. We encourage you to take the time to begin with the best practice outlined in Chapter 3: *Know your own thoughts and feelings.* Death by suicide will leave you reeling. Those caught in a suicide's wake can feel a web of thoughts and emotions: shock, sadness, anger, shame, frustration, fear, confusion, relief, powerlessness, loneliness, guilt, and numbness, among others. Try to sift through and acknowledge your feelings before you sit with your child, knowing that all your feelings are valid. Perhaps speak with a friend or partner, a therapist or religious advisor, or write down your thoughts; take a walk if you can to clear your head a little. Your goal is to be able to tell your child without imposing your own thoughts or emotions on them. Remember that young children will take in your body language almost as much as the words you say, so be aware of what you communicate even in a non-verbal way.

When you are as ready as you can be, find a private space and time to share the news. You want to be sure that you won't be interrupted and that you have enough time to sit with your child afterward. At its essence, we feel that telling children about a suicide should be done in two parts: the first is that the death has occurred, and the second, more complicated part is that the person ended their own life. There may be several hours or a day or two between the two conversations, depending on your child's developmental understanding and whether there is the likelihood that she might find out from someone else. Remember that young people often turn to texting and social media to talk, and news can spread rapidly.

TAKEAWAY
First tell your child that the person has died, then if your child is older than six, have a separate conversation to say they ended their own life.

If you have more than one child and one is younger than six, we recommend sharing the news about the death together as a family and then having a separate conversation about the nature of the death later with your older child.

For breaking the news, we recommend starting with something such as, "We have some sad news to share. We learned that Grandpa died this morning."

Depending on your child's reactions or questions, you might share the cause of his death by following the best practices *Don't keep secrets* and *Tell the truth, nothing but the truth but not the whole truth—at least not all at once*: "His heart stopped working," or "His car hit a tree and his body was hurt too much to work anymore." Here, you would omit details that would show that he had ended his own life, the fact that he took a concoction of pills that caused his heart to stop, or that he drove the car into a tree on purpose. As you close your conversation, let your child know that you will check in with her again soon and that you are always available for any questions that may come up.

In opening the second conversation with your child, again make sure you find privacy and an extended period of time that you can spend together. Your aim is to give your child the truth in language that she can understand, while providing reassurance and security that you are there to help her with the news. You might start the conversation with something along the lines of, "I told you earlier that Grandpa died today and that we are all feeling sad about the news. I want to tell you a little more. He died because his heart stopped. But he made this happen by taking too many pills. He ended his own life."

As your child takes in the news, you could add, "We call this suicide." We recommend that you use the words "death by suicide," "died by suicide," "ended her own life," or "took his own life." We feel the words "she killed herself" are overly graphic, and the phrase "he committed suicide" is antiquated and negative.

While the language you use may vary, we believe that acknowledging your child's confusion is an important part. You could say, "This may seem confusing. It's sometimes hard for grown-ups to understand, too."

Your child may not have the words to ask questions or know how she feels and so she might greet the news in silence. Be aware that she may have many emotions and thoughts—some contradictory—buzzing inside her, and she might need your help in expressing them.

Bear in mind the best practice *Expect the unexpected* and be ready for any and all reactions. You know best what may help your child in this moment, whether it is holding her hand, offering a hug, or sitting quietly. Your role is to provide love and reassurance for your child in the face of something disturbing.

Let your child know that she may ask any questions she has now or that come to her later, saying, "I'm here to answer any questions. I may not always know the answers, but I will do my best to find out."

In many cases, a child may not tell you the way she is feeling, especially if she is embarrassed, ashamed, or feeling relief about the death. In the hours and days that follow breaking the news, you can help her to name her internal experience and let her know that all her feelings are valid. By asking, "What are you thinking about this?" or "How is this sitting with you?" you invite your child to open up. You could be on the lookout for behavioral reactions and assist her in putting names to emotions she's showing in words or actions: "Is it possible that you're feeling angry?" or "I hear you blaming yourself, but this is not your fault."

If you have a child under the age of six who asks a direct question about whether the person ended their own life, perhaps because they overheard someone, then you are compelled to answer truthfully. We recommend a brief confirmation and then suggest you follow our advice for children aged six and older—while being sensitive to her young age.

Common Questions

Why?

In our experience, the most common question that children ask about a death by suicide is "Why?" They may form this question on hearing the news or later as they begin to process the death. We believe it is helpful to promote compassion in your child's understanding of why a death occurred and recommend talking about it in terms of a disease—suicidality—and to describe it as the result of a tragic loss of hope. Many people who take their own lives struggle with a mental health disorder, especially depression, but there can often be other underlying factors involved. It is important, therefore, to explain that suicide is complicated and to emphasize that the person who died was experiencing overwhelming emotional pain that made it hard to consider other options. When you present suicide in this way you can help to remove the stigma around it, making it less likely that the deceased is blamed for taking his own life. You might use language such as, "We don't know why, for sure, but Grandpa struggled with a disease called depression for a long time. It made him feel kind of empty and sad. It's a different sadness than you or I know. It meant that he thought he couldn't enjoy life anymore. He couldn't see the ways to feel better that were there," or "We can't really know exactly why Mrs. Garcia took her own life. There probably isn't just one reason, except she must have thought that dying was the only option for her. She wasn't able to see the way forward that is always there."

When you speak about suicide as an illness, it lets you reinforce with your child that there are treatments available for suicidal feelings, that suicide is not the solution to emotional torment, and that there are ways to ease the pain and find hope again. You might say, "I'm sad that your uncle struggled so much and that he ended his own life. I wish he had gone for treatment." You could also say, "I wish that your uncle had told someone he was feeling so hopeless and we could have helped him to find treatment." This could open up a conversation that you are always available to listen to your child's questions and needs, and ready to help if she ever feels hopeless herself—and that sharing a problem with someone else can make it easier to work through it.

Didn't He Love Me Enough to Live?

Many children worry that their loved one didn't care enough about them to stay alive. "Didn't Mommy love me?" or "Didn't he know I would miss him?" could be answered with: "Your mom loved you very much but she had a disease that meant that she couldn't feel hope or happiness anymore, and made her think incorrectly that you and I and everyone who knew her would be better off if she died," or "You meant the world to your big brother but he had an illness in his brain that made living too hard and he didn't see the hope or help that was there for him." You would aim to reassure your child that they were cherished and that an illness caused the person who died to end his life, and that these two statements can both be true.

Was It My Fault?

Some young children believe that their thoughts or words can cause someone to end their life. Or think that if they had done something different they could have kept the person alive. This kind of thinking can lead to feelings of shame and guilt. It's vital that you let your child know that nothing she said or did—or didn't say or do—could have made someone end his own life.

A few years ago Elena worked with Daniela, mother of twin eight-year-olds Liam and Josh, whose husband took his own life by jumping from a bridge. She turned to Elena to sort out her own emotions and how to help her sons through this sudden loss. She was blindsided by the suicide and leaned upon her brother to sit with her and tell her sons the news that their father had died after falling from a height. The next morning, again with her brother's help, she told them the whole truth: that their father had jumped to his death. She explained that he had struggled with a disease that changed the way he thought and it had meant he couldn't see any hope in his world or in his future, that he didn't think he was ever going to feel good again, and that the only way to not feel this pain was to die. Understandably, her sons were devastated. "Didn't he care that we loved him?" asked Liam. Daniela's brother answered, "He loved you both so much but when you have this sickness, the pain overwhelms all hope. He had this wrong idea that you would be better off without him in the world."

The boys struggled with their father's death, finding it hard to go to sleep and making their way into Daniela's bed in the middle of the night. Liam often woke up screaming and drenched in sweat. Josh started fights with his brother, kicking him or punching him without provocation. Daniela was exhausted by her own grief but she listened to her boys. "Maybe you are mad at Daddy for leaving us," she told Josh, suspecting his new outward aggression mirrored his internal confusion and resentment. "I am mad at the disease that took him away."

Over the years, with Elena's help, Daniela revisited the story of her husband's death with her sons, and her brother remained a strong presence in their life, ready to listen to and answer their questions. Recently, the boys turned twelve, and Daniela added another strand to their understanding of their father's death: that a family history of suicide is considered a risk factor for suicide in a related family member. She explained that this knowledge could be a protective factor for them as she, they, and their doctors could be alert to any warning signs. She talked with them about creating a pact that they would come to her if they were ever feeling hopeless or despairing, and that they could count on her to respond with love and understanding, and to support them in getting any help they might need.

Daniela's sons had developed close bonds with their mother. They trusted her to tell them the truth and knew they could go to her with any question. This trust, this bond, was hard-won.

Later in the chapter, we'll elaborate on ways to build on the foundation of trust you are creating with your own child and show how it can safeguard her in the future.

We know that a parent's first instinct is to protect their child. To us, that means speaking the truth, helping your child to understand, and supporting her as she asks questions and expresses emotions. Your child will see with your guidance that even the most heartrending situation can be faced.

When Suicide Touches Your Child's Life from Afar

Though we wish it were not so, it is likely that your young child's world will be impacted by suicide in some way, if not on a personal level, and we believe it is helpful for you to have an understanding of how to talk together on the subject when it happens. Throughout this book, we speak about conversation as the cornerstone of the parent-child relationship and we advocate for starting daily chats and check-ins early with your child on topics large and small. The more you can do this—and it's never too late to start—the easier it is to talk about something as unnerving as suicide. In this next section, we will help you to assess whether to talk to your child about a suicide on the periphery of her world, and, if necessary, how to do so.

TAKEAWAY

It is best to proactively talk to your child about a suicide they are likely to hear about, even if the person is not close to them or is in the media.

Death by suicide is becoming increasingly common at the school-age level and your child may hear about a suicide within her school community. News travels fast via text and social media among young people, school networks, and between friends and siblings of different ages, and the report of a suicide in a middle school or high school is likely to ripple outward and reach the ears of children in elementary school.

Your child may not know exactly what the words mean but she will understand that something terrible has happened. In a similar manner, when a celebrity or person of note dies by suicide, your child may see and/or hear news coverage of the death and be aware that it is a subject of discussion on the edges of her life. Likewise, some young children find out about suicide through movies and television shows with story lines about suicide aimed at teenagers, such as *13 Reasons Why* and *All the Bright Places*. Your child may overhear older siblings, family members, and friends discussing them, or she may search out the shows herself, curious to find out more, or may stumble upon them by mistake. However it happens, this exposure to suicide among young children is not uncommon.

One of Michael's patients said to him, "My seven-year-old asked me point-blank about suicide. We were on our way to the dentist. He asked as if it were the most natural question in the world." It turned out that her son had heard her and her twelve-year-old daughter discussing a musician's suicide. "I should have guessed he would know something about it. It's been all over the news." Your child may come to you with questions if suicide has impacted her world in some way—especially if you have a relationship in which you communicate a lot with each other. With your usual after-school questions and the to-and-fro of conversations, she might raise the topic. However, many children will not ask questions at all, so it is important to be attentive to your child's behavior to give her a chance to show you in some way and be ready to broach the subject.

If you decide that you should talk to your child, we recommend finding a comfortable and private spot at home and making sure that you have enough time to ensure the conversation is not rushed. First, try to find out what your child already knows so that you don't engulf him in too much information. He only needs to hear simple, honest statements from you, enough to help him to understand what has happened without overwhelming him. You might say, "Have you heard anyone talking about the TV show *13 Reasons Why*? I know some of the older kids at school have been watching it," or "Your sister and I were having a conversation about an actor who died this week. I wonder if you heard and if you have any questions?" If a suicide has happened in the local school community, you might ask, "What's new at school today?" If it seems that your child has not heard anything and doesn't need to talk, then you could drop the subject (while remaining attentive).

If your child *is* aware of talk around a death by suicide, you would want to find out if she knows the term "suicide" and what it means. You could give a brief explanation: suicide is when people feel they do not want to be alive anymore because they can't see any of the available hope and so they do something very harmful to cause themselves to die. By figuring out what your child knows, you can enter the conversation in the same place, or meet your child where she is, and then build on her knowledge. This is a good time to teach your child that suicide is very hard to understand; it is okay to feel a lot of emotions when someone dies by suicide; it is not usually the result of one particular thing (like losing a job or a relationship ending); and that many people who die by suicide struggled with a mental health condition. You might say, "Sadly, some people have a disease that makes them feel such hopelessness that they don't think they will ever get better, and they think that death is the only way to end that pain," or "Sometimes people have an illness that makes them feel trapped and hopeless, that the world would be a better place without them in it, and it is hard for them to think clearly or to get help."

It is also a time to communicate that you wish the person who died had received treatment that worked for him, or had found ways to feel that there were other solutions to his emotional pain than death. "The boy in the movie felt stuck and overwhelmed by everything and thought that dying was the best solution. I wish he had told someone how he was feeling and they could have helped him to find a treatment."

TAKEAWAY
Convey to your child that there is always a way through any problem or feeling and you will be there to help them navigate it.

While speaking with your young child about someone taking their own life may seem excruciating, in our experience we have found that children who learn about suicide in a thoughtful conversation with a parent are bolstered by the experience, that honesty and truth delivered in a caring way make them feel secure.

One of Michael's patients told him that her teenage son had come to her on Saturday morning and said he needed to talk. He told his mom that a friend of his seemed really down, that she was saying how no one would miss her if she weren't around, and maybe it would be better for everyone if she were dead. He wasn't sure what to do. The mom had sympathized with him, saying how hard that must have been to hear, and how glad she was that he had come to her for help. Together they came up with a plan to tell an adult in his friend's life so that she could start to get the help she needed.

Many teens we work with tell us that they wouldn't discuss suicide with their parents because the subject makes their parents anxious—but they also say that they want to talk about it because, for better or worse, it's part of their lives.

Talking to your child about suicide at a young age when necessary plants the seed that she can come to you with questions about anything and everything, that no subject is taboo, and that you will listen to what she has to say. The more you have discussions with her on topics of all kinds as she grows up, the more you open pathways to future talks. As you do, both you and your child will feel more comfortable and prepared for the conversations about mental health and suicide that will be essential as your child enters middle school and high school. At that time, you would want to communicate:

o   I am always available for you to ask me about anything

o   I will listen and not judge

o   I will help you

o   Speaking about worries can be one step toward making things better

o   Speaking with someone brings connection and eases isolation

o   Through conversation, we can find that others feel the same way we do

o   Speaking to someone about suicide will not lead that person toward suicide

o   If you tell someone that a friend is suicidal, the friend may be angry at first but will be grateful later

o   Conversations about suicide can save someone's life

The importance of speaking to your child about suicide comes full circle here: by talking with him about it when he is young, you create a bond that grows over time until, one day, if he—or a friend—is feeling suicidal, he knows he can trust you to listen and help. In these instances, your child's ability to have a difficult conversation with you—and you with him—can be a lifesaver.

Chapter 12

Talking to Your Child About Death in the Media

✻ Processing Your Own Reaction ✻ Telling Your Child ✻

✻ Look for the Helpers ✻ Minimize TV and Social Media ✻

✻ Talking About Safety ✻ Answering "Why Did It Happen?" ✻

✻ Discussing Violence ✻ Managing Anger ✻

✻ Overcoming Helplessness ✻ Ongoing Reactions ✻

With twenty-four-hour news cycles and easy access to the Internet and social media, even young children are exposed on a regular basis to gun violence, homicides, acts of terror, opioid overdose deaths, natural disasters, and other tragic events that claim the lives of many. We live in an age of anxiety where kindergartners practice lockdown drills, and the media broadcasts daily alarming images of death and destruction from all across the globe. In these ways, children receive the message that death can be everywhere and that the world is not always a safe place to be. It is hard to shield young ears from this information—though many would like to do so—and we believe it is best if you can talk honestly with your child about death in the media as a way to help him to process it and cope. In this chapter, our aim is to guide you through situations in which you may feel saddened, anxious, confused, or at a loss for words because of happenings in the world at large: we will provide you with language to meet the needs of your child.

Whether it's a mass shooting or a natural disaster that is filling the news, it's safe for you as a parent to assume that your child—even at the age of three—has taken in information, at some level, that something worrying is going on in the world. Often children glean information as parents watch television or catch up on current events on computers, unaware that their young child is absorbing it, too. Children may overhear adults talking about a situation or they may notice that their parents seem scared or worried, or that they stop talking or turn off the TV when the child enters the room. This can all be unsettling to a young child. As we have said in previous chapters, silence around a subject can make it even more frightening in your child's mind as he wonders what could be so terrible that it can't even be discussed. Your reticence around a topic may cause your child to turn to friends, older siblings, or other media sources for information. In the end, your desire to protect your child from unpleasant news leaves him alone with the disturbing truth, or his own distorted narrative.

Many parents tell us that they don't want to upset their children with bad news. We understand this inclination to shield your child. However, we think it's important for you to bear in mind that it is the news of the event that may upset your child, not that you are telling him. In fact, when you make the decision to share the news, you have an opportunity to guide your child through his distress by telling him the truth and supporting his reactions, by showing him that you are there for him. This is a gift.

When a tragedy hits and is all over the news, we believe it's time to prepare a conversation, as your child likely either will ask direct questions or will have questions in his mind that he may need help putting into words.

Process Your Own Emotional Response First

We recommend that you take some time to know how you feel before you speak with your child about a shocking or upsetting event or incident. In Chapter 3, we elaborate on this best practice: *Know your own thoughts and feelings*. Sometimes we are unaware of how emotionally affected we are by something until we start to talk to someone else, and then the tears, anxiety, or anger emerge. It's best if you can have your first reaction away from your child. It can be difficult to see your own child's anguish, especially when you are overwrought yourself, and your conversation with her will be a little easier for you if you have grounded yourself first. It will also enable you to focus outward, to empathize with your child and to address her needs, rather than look inward toward your own reaction. If your child is with you when you learn of an event, you may have to settle her with an activity she can do on her own and take some time for yourself, even just for a few minutes.

o   Try to understand which emotions you are feeling

   You might be sad, angry, overwhelmed, scared, helpless, or wor-
   ried. Perhaps confused by many feelings. Or in a state of numb-
   ness or shock

o   Try to understand why you are feeling this way

   Perhaps you are sad for the victims who have died and for their
   families

   You might be angry if people have died at the hands of others

   You may be worried and scared about your loved ones' safety

   Maybe you are overwhelmed by so much loss, or by the idea of
   evil or injustice in the world

   You could be thinking about the wider implications of an event
   in society and wanting to do something about it

   It's possible that the event has stirred up memories of other
   deaths for you, personal or public, and the emotions and grief
   surrounding them

o   Try to find ways to manage your emotions

   Talk to a friend or partner, or write things down

   Go for a walk, exercise, throw a ball against a wall, or shoot
   some hoops

   Try some breathing exercises

   Listen to uplifting or loud music

   Take a break from the news and social media

   Talk with a trusted professional, or a mentor, or a religious
   advisor

For adults, a tragedy in the news can bring a multitude of thoughts and feelings that ripple outward from the loss at the center. When the headlines bring news of the death of a person of color at the hands of police, you could be stirred emotionally in many ways, perhaps intensely so, on a personal and political level. You may grapple with thoughts about the safety of your own family, and the underlying reasons for why it has happened. Depending on the age of your child, you might want to have extended conversations on these subjects, even later the same day, but when breaking the news you should keep to the specifics of the event.

A school shooting may be upsetting to you as you think about young lives destroyed and families devastated, but it may also bring up other issues for you: perhaps reflections on why these shootings occur, the level of safety at your child's school, worries about your own security at work, and concerns about protecting your loved ones. Your child does not need to know all this, especially in the initial telling.

Before you have your conversation, come up with a sentence or two, the simpler the better, that encapsulates the news you would like to share. What message would you like your child to hear? We recommend a simple statement of the facts, some reassurance about the outcome, and some loving words of comfort. For example, "There was a very big wave that came out of the ocean and into a town in a country far away from here. Some people died but many people were not hurt. People all over the world are helping, and scientists are looking for ways to stop it from happening again. You are safe here with me." While you might not say all this at once or in exactly this way, these are the basic elements that you would want your child to know.

TAKEAWAY
Emphasize to your child what is being done to prevent this from happening again.

Breaking the News

Depending on your child, he may come to you with questions about something happening in the news or he may not. If he does, it is a good idea to sit somewhere private and have a thoughtful conversation rather than answering questions on the fly. If you are in the middle of a task or away from home, you may need to say something such as, "I'm glad you asked me and I'd like to answer your question. Let's finish up at the store and we'll talk about it when we get home."

If your child does not ask questions and you decide to initiate a conversation, it is best to find a time and place when you can be ready for his reactions and stay with him as he takes in the news.

In both cases, when you talk to your child, we recommend that you gauge what he already knows and what he might be ready to know, instead of launching into an explanation of events. You might say, "At the grocery store, you asked me about the plane that crashed in Chicago. What did you hear about it?" or, if he hasn't asked questions, "There has been a lot of news and talk about something that happened. I want to let you know what that is. Have you heard people talking about a new thing that happened?"

If your child confirms that he has, ask him what he knows about the event. This will help you to know if he has accurate information and whether he has misunderstandings or has heard frightening rumors. It is best if you can let him speak before correcting his misperceptions so that he has a chance to tell you everything.

If your child says he has not heard about the event but you feel it is very likely that he will do so, then we recommend breaking the news in clear, age-appropriate language. Your child will be able to cope better with a situation if he understands it. For a natural disaster, you might say, "There is sad news today about an event that happened to some people we do not know. A big windstorm broke some buildings and some people died. The rescue teams saved a lot of other people and they are home and safe." Or, for a mass shoot-ing, "Today a sad thing happened at a shopping mall far away from here. Someone used a gun to kill some people. The other people are safe now and first responders are doing their job to help stop it from happening again." Your goal is to tell your child the truth while reas-suring him that the event is over and that right now the two of you are together and okay.

After this initial statement, you could ask your child if he has any questions. Some children may want more details about what happened and you could answer in a similar way, providing simple explanations. Take your cues from your child in determining how much information to provide. By listening carefully to the language he uses and the feedback he gives you, you'll know what to say next, and also when your child does not want to hear more. It's helpful to remember that this is likely to be an ongoing conversation and your child may want to know more over time—be sure to let him know that you are available for any and all of his questions that occur to him later. You may also say that you don't know in response to your child's questions if you don't have all the facts—it's okay not to know everything. You might say that as new information emerges you will let him know—and you should make sure you follow up with him as you learn more. However, we do not suggest misleading your child or covering up what you do know. Later in the chapter we pro-vide answers to common questions.

Your Child's Emotional Response

Your child's reaction to the news will be dependent on her age, her personality, and her prior experience with and exposure to death. Her response may surprise you or not, but we advise you to be ready for anything. Your child may have an immediate emotional response as you give her the news, perhaps tearing up or crying, or she may say that she doesn't like what you've told her, that it makes her scared or mad. Or she may not outwardly react. Encourage her to try to communicate with you what she is feeling inside, letting her know that it's okay and natural to feel lots of different emotions all at once, or to feel nothing at all. You might say, "How is this sitting with you?" Or, "What do you think about it?"

We would recommend that you do not focus on your own fears and anxieties—though it is likely that you may be struggling with them. You could say something along the lines of, "It made some people feel nervous at first and some people are angry, but everyone is finding ways to take in the news." Your child will look to you for reassurance so it's best to convey a sense that things will be okay, even if it doesn't seem that way in the moment.

Focus on the Positive

While it may be difficult for you to see anything other than unre-mitting despair about a tragedy, when you break the news to your child, it's really helpful to her if you can balance the sadness of the events with positive stories of people who rushed in to assist victims and survivors, and are continuing to do so. This allows her to realize that there can be good even in the midst of something terrible. You can let your child know that many people and organizations, both at the scene of the tragedy and around the world, are joining together to try to make the situation better. This is likely to remind you, too, to take a moment and think beyond the bleak news. Fred Rogers, the wise and gentle host of *Mister Rogers' Neighborhood*, often told the story that when he saw scary news on TV as a child, his mother would always say, "Look for the helpers." It was something he continued to do throughout his life, and wisdom he shared with generations of parents. We would agree that adding an additional lens as you think of the incident and looking for goodness, for hope, in the midst of darkness is beneficial for children and adults alike.

Limit Access to TV/Media

We recommend you keep your child away from the news as much as possible in the immediate aftermath of a calamitous event, not to prevent him from finding out more, but to be able to modulate what new information he takes in and to try to stop him from seeing distressful images that will embed themselves in his mind far longer than words. Some young children believe that an event is happening all over again each time they see a replay, thus setting off new—and cumulative—emotional responses on each viewing. It is best that you explain to your child your reasons for preventing or limiting access to the TV or (depending on your child's age) social media and reiterating that if he has more questions about the event at any time he may ask and you will answer truthfully. For your school-age child, you may not have complete control over what he sees on television or online, as he is not always under your care or in the family home. We believe it is a good idea to tell your child that you would prefer him not to view news footage without you because you think it is important that you be with him to help him sort it out. You could assist him in coming up with language that he can use at a friend's house if he feels pressured to watch: "I don't really want to see that. It makes me sad."

If, despite your best efforts to limit access, your child does happen to catch sight of disturbing images, try not to berate yourself. What is most important is that you can help your child to process what he has seen and that will diminish the negative impact. We also recommend that you try to counteract the upsetting images with positive images from the event: look to the helpers again.

Common Questions

Over the years, as we have helped children and parents process senseless violence, tragic happenings, and mass deaths brought into their homes via the media, there are two questions that come up time and again:

Could That Happen to Me?

For most children, the news of a frightening and upsetting event may elicit feelings of sadness or shock, but their underlying primary concern is "Could that happen to me?" "Could that happen to my family?" Another way of thinking about these questions is "Am I safe?" or "Are we safe?" If your child tells you he is scared, it is important to validate his feelings rather than rushing to reassure him. Telling him, "You're fine! Don't worry about it!" will not make anxious thoughts magically disappear. Instead, honest discussion helps your child to feel supported by you and grounded in his trust for you.

We are aware that keeping your child safe means different things to different people and that having the ability to do so may not be possible. As in other conversations, we recommend telling your child the truth and staying within the bounds of what is age-appropriate. If you feel that your child's safety may be compromised because of the color of her skin, ethnicity, cultural background, or religion, then we urge you to talk to your child about it while finding ways to convey how you and she can maximize safety.

We have found that it is best to let your child know that you are doing your very best to keep him safe and to give him concrete examples of how you go about doing this. The aim is not to pretend that danger doesn't exist but to reassure your child that you are doing everything you can to be prepared for whatever may happen. "We keep the windows and doors locked to our house." "We have fire alarms in our home and change the batteries often." "Your school has a safety plan in place." "We have a list of phone numbers on the fridge to call if there's an emergency." It is also helpful to remind your child that there are lots of people in his life who are keeping him safe—you, his family members, friends, teachers, and neighbors. You could include others such as firefighters, first responders, nurses, doctors, or law enforcement officers as you feel appropriate.

If you live in a place where certain natural disasters do occur, it's best to acknowledge this reality with your child rather than brushing it away. You might say, "It's very unlikely that our neighborhood will be in a tornado but we do have a safety plan in place, just in case. We have a plan to all go to the basement together, and we have extra food, water, flashlights, and blankets down there in case we ever need them."

One of Michael's friends found her four-year-old daughter preparing a survival kit of food and water for herself and the family dog after seeing news coverage of serious flooding in a distant part of the country. While talking about the floods and explaining to her daughter that they didn't need to worry as they lived on the eighth floor of an apartment building, the mother praised her resourcefulness. It opened up a conversation about safety, and together mother and daughter created a first aid kit of Band-Aids and antibiotic ointment and a snack pack of granola bars and dog treats to keep on hand for future outings. "It seemed like a simple way to show that we can be prepared for something that may happen like a skinned knee or hunger pangs while not worrying about events that are beyond our control." As her daughter grows older, she'll continue to address other aspects of how she can keep herself safe.

When talking to your child about his safety after a traumatic event, it can be helpful to let him know that the event in question does not happen very often if that is true—which is one reason why it is being talked about on the news so much. You could say that every single day thousands of airplanes fly from place to place without crashing, if an airline disaster is filling the news, or that many, many music concerts take place every day all around the world without a bomb exploding there. Knowing that catastrophes are not the norm can help your child gain perspective.

Public tragedies remind us of the vulnerability of life and it is easy to feel shaken and scared. While you may be thinking that it is impossible to be completely secure all of the time, or to guarantee your child's safety, she does not need to know that right then. She needs your reassurance and extra emotional support after such events, so take the time to encourage her about what she can feel secure about in her world and to let her know that her loved ones are out of harm's way, if that is true. You may feel the need to reiterate ways she can keep herself safe. You can also sit and read or watch a favorite movie, and just be around each other. You could make a call to loved ones so your child knows that they are okay. "Grandma just finished her dinner, too, and is about to go to the store!" "Aunt Ruthie just got home from work and she and Uncle Noah say hi." Try to show that the small world she knows is still going on.

Why Did It Happen?

Young children are inveterate scientists and are innately curious about the world around them, seeking to make sense of it through questions and observations. Their reaction to terrible events in the news is no different: they often ask why something happened. "Why did the hurricane kill all those people?" "Why did someone shoot the kids at their school?" We know that such questions are likely to bring a flood of responses to your mind and it can be hard to know where to start, how much to say, or what exactly to say, especially when your natural instinct might be to try to say nothing at all. It's important to remember that your child's why is likely not the same as the why that you may be asking. We would again counsel you to keep things simple, while telling the truth.

For natural disasters such as hurricanes, floods, tornadoes, earthquakes, tsunamis, etc., you can explain that they are forces of nature, and it isn't possible to prevent them from happening. "There was so much rain that it made the river fill with extra water that went into people's houses and some people died." While answering such questions, it is always helpful to counterbalance the news of multiple deaths with the reminder that many other people were saved. "Scientists and people who know a lot about weather thought that there would be flooding and warned people ahead of time. A lot of people got out of their houses in time and are fine now and being looked after."

When someone shoots a group of schoolchildren or bombs a building causing many people to die, you might find yourself at a loss for words. It's not easy to explain to ourselves why one person might decide to kill other people, and it is especially difficult to try to enlighten a child. For some young children, their first exposure to the idea of good and evil in the world comes as they absorb the language, themes, and plots of fairy tales and children's movies. They know all about the wicked queen who sends Snow White into the woods to perish and *The Little Mermaid*'s malicious trickster, Ursula. It's not news for them that people can have ill intent toward others. Other children learn this harsh reality in their own lives from an early age. When violence erupts in the real world—her own world— your child is very likely to ask the question why.

First, we recommend that you tell your child that you appreciate her asking the question, to send her the message that even if the subject matter is difficult, questions and conversation are always welcome. Be sure to acknowledge that some situations are hard to understand, even for grown-ups, and that sometimes things happen that don't make any sense and don't fit with our view of what is right and wrong. When speaking about the reasons for violence perpetrated by one human against another, we suggest you say something along the lines of, "We don't know for sure why someone used a gun to kill students at that school. It's a terrible and sad thing. But some people are so angry that they take out their anger on others to hurt them."

You might let your child know that it is okay for him to be mad at the person or people responsible while helping him to express those feelings in appropriate ways. "When I feel mad, I just have to get moving. That might calm you, too," or "When some people are upset they like to be with their friends or go to church or play loud music." The more you can help your child to name and express his feelings, the more he will be able to manage those feelings of anger in productive ways that are not harmful to himself or others.

It is also important to model for your child that blaming certain people or ethnic groups in response to violence is not helpful. There is an important difference between feeling anger toward the perpetrator of a violent act and feeling that same fury toward all who share the same ethnicity or background. Or toward all people who struggle with mental illness. Instead, you might suggest that the aftermath of a tragic event is a time to be especially thoughtful about being kind to and inclusive of others in an attempt to heal.

Your child may find it difficult to handle the uncertainty of not knowing for sure why something happened, or whether it might happen again. Giving her the tools to cope with ambiguity and doubt can help her throughout her life. Let her know that talking about things, no matter how uneasy it makes her feel, can help, as can sitting in silence with someone she loves so she knows she is not going through this experience alone. Support comes in the form of being in it together. While she may not be able to take comfort in knowing why something happened, she can perhaps find solace in knowing that other people also don't know and this uncomfortable feeling is shared.

How to Combat Feelings of Helplessness

Many of us feel helpless in the face of news about violence or in response to things that seem so much bigger than we are and beyond our control. Just as talking about finding the helpers enables your child to look beyond the immediate sorrow of a tragedy, taking concrete actions as a family to donate money, supplies, or time can give your child a way to feel less overwhelmed while doing some good. If your child wishes she could have changed what happened, let her know that this is a natural reaction, one that many people may share. You could suggest that you and your child think about what might be done now to help, saying something along the lines of, "I wish I could change what happened with the hurricane but I can't. But I am going to donate some money that will buy food and clothing for the victims' families." Here you would be modeling compassion to your child, empathy in action. If you think your child is old enough, she could brainstorm with you about different options to help and ways that she can get involved. Perhaps she could help pick out clothes and food to donate. Or write a card to the people affected.

You could also talk to your child about trying to create positive change, perhaps by working to put in place laws or protocols or to raise awareness so that it can be harder for a similar tragedy to happen again. "I am so mad about what happened and I'm going to tell our government so they can make laws to prevent it in the future. I'm going to write letters to Congress." Actions speak louder than words, so let your child know what you and other family members are doing to help. This is another good way of showing your child that she has a choice in how to manage whatever she may feel. You are your child's most powerful learning tool. When you model constructive coping strategies, you enable your child to become more resilient as she learns how to handle feeling helpless herself.

Ongoing Feelings and Coping Mechanisms

When there is a tragedy in the news, it is a natural reaction for you and your child to be upset. In our experience, we have found that common responses to disasters for young children include:

o   Separation anxiety and clinginess

o   Changes to sleep patterns and not wanting to sleep alone

o   Hitting or fighting

o   Bedwetting

o   Fidgeting

You may find that your child's anxiety about the event and the fear that it could happen to him manifest as him wanting to stay at home or to be near you constantly, especially at bedtime. Every child is different and will respond to tragic events in the media in his own way, but in general you should see these reactions lessen within a few weeks. If the fear and anxiety continue for a while, and seem to be impacting your child's life, it may be time to talk to your child's teacher, pediatrician, or a mental health professional for advice. In the meantime, patience and calm reassurance from you will be helpful at this time, as will keeping your child's routines as regular as possible. Your aim is to wrap him in security and love as he wrestles with the knowledge that the world can be a scary place at times—while sending him the message that your connection through conversation is constant.

Chapter 13

A Death Within the Immediate Family: Specific and Practical Support

---

❋ When a Parent or Parent Figure Has Died ❋

❋ When Your Child's Sibling Has Died ❋

❋ When a Close Family Member Has Died by Suicide ❋

❋ When You Are Grieving the Loss of an Expected Baby: Miscarriage or Stillbirth ❋

I f someone extremely close to you and your child has died, we are aware that you may be devastated. Agony like this can leave you in darkness as you try to wrap your mind around the loss. You might be feeling shock, sadness, anger, and confusion, a tumult of thoughts and emotions that have left you overwhelmed. You could be worried that you have so many things to do, that you have to take care of your child in the midst of it all, and that you don't know where to begin. You are not alone. Our hope is to offer here tailored guidance and practical solutions to help you through this difficult time.

o   The immediate impact of this death will be greater as it touches your life in concrete as well as emotional ways. Acknowledging this fact may help you give the time and space needed to manage the loss.

o   Assigning a "point person" or "point people" is essential to streamline the burden placed on you by the death. Someone to field requests, messages, and condolences, and take charge of—and delegate—the handling of practical arrangements can help to create a sanctuary of sorts for you and your child.

o   It is particularly important to try to take care of yourself. While it may feel impossible to grab even a moment for yourself, any extra support you can find for your own emotional needs will help you to attend to your child.

o   Your child is likely to worry that you will die. Be ready to answer her questions honestly and to provide her with reassurance and comfort in the form of hugs and being with her as much as possible.

o   Your child may be afraid she will lose you emotionally, too, so your strong, steady presence is one of the most heartening things you can provide for her. The more you can show your child that you are able to function and have healthy ways of coping, the more relieved she will feel.

○ Help your child to see there are other people in her life who care for her. You might include family members, friends, teachers, babysitters, neighbors, etc., to show a vast world of kind people in her orbit. Make sure she knows how to contact them if necessary.

○ Your child might need more days at home with you before returning to usual activities, but the goal is still to engage in life and stay with routine as much as possible—your child will find it grounding and reassuring to have structure in her world.

○ Close collaboration with your child's school or childcare is essential as you set up a caring environment for her when she is away from you. It may take a few days to get a plan in action, but it will likely make you feel more comfortable in sending your child back, which may provide you with relief. We provide general guidelines in Chapter 9 and, as your child may be more vulnerable at this time, we offer additional suggestions here to help you prepare. Some can apply to childcare situations other than school:

> *Before your child's return, arrange for her to speak with her teacher by phone or video call so that she can hear that everyone is ready to welcome her back.*

> *Arrange for your child to meet with her teacher one-on-one on her first day back, before school starts, if possible.*

> *Have the school tell each class about your child's loss, including the cause of death if publicly known, so that she does not feel the need to explain herself.*

Identify a school friend as a supportive helper for your child.

Give your child words with which to respond when people ask about her loved one's death or speak to her about it. "Yes, my daddy died." "Yes, my sister died." Role-play with her a few times so that she can feel more comfortable in using these words.

Let her know that she can say as much as she wishes—or nothing at all—and help her come up with a way to say, "I don't feel like talking about it."

Make sure she knows which grown-up to turn to for support during her school day.

Plan to be in regular touch with your child's teacher (and ask that the teacher reach out to you) once your child has returned and in the weeks that follow to provide a net of support and communication for your child.

o Let your child know that you'll be checking in with her over time on how she's doing, that sometimes she'll feel like talking with you and at other times she won't. In this way, your questions will be part of the process and will not make her worry or suggest that you have concerns.

o Be aware of your new family constellation, as your family unit will look different going forward. Acknowledge the change and validate your child's and possibly your own feelings about it: "We're still a family, just a different-shaped family now."

o Seek professional help. It can be helpful for both you and your child. Even if your child is not showing signs of struggling in the face of her loss, we believe it is beneficial for her to talk to and have the support of a professional, such as her pediatrician, school counselor, a therapist or grief counselor, or a member of your religious institution. If, four to six weeks after the death, she is finding it difficult to engage in her regular activities, we strongly recommend that you reach out for professional help.

Even with guidance you may still feel overwrought. If you can try to keep your thoughts and actions small and concrete, in the here and now, you may find your mind is calmer. Try not to look at the big picture today but focus on making it through each hour. Ask yourself, What do I need now? What am I able to do now? And let's take it from there together.

When a Parent or Parent Figure Has Died

The loss of a parent or parent figure can be one of the most upsetting events in a child's life. While many family units have different structures and components, we understand that the death of your child's parent is likely to mean that your spouse or partner (current or former) has died and that this may be a terribly difficult time for you. We offer here some specific pointers.

o   You may find that you're more anxious than ever before. This is a natural reaction to feeling more responsibility, now that your co-parent is no longer there, and to concerns about how your child may cope with the loss. An awareness of this emotion can give you some perspective on it, which can ease your discomfort. It can also give you insight into where you feel most vulnerable and where you need most support.

o   Your child is likely to ask if you will die, too. Reassure your child with an answer along the lines of: "I take very good care of my health and I'm planning to live for a long time." Being present with your child will comfort her, too.

o   Your child's return to school or childcare will need your attention, as it is best to let him get back to the supportive structure of his usual daily activities sooner rather than later. We recommend you follow our general guidelines in Chapter 9 and our additional suggestions on pages 203–4. Here we offer advice that may apply to your specific situation:

> *Over time, work with teachers to scope ahead for school events (such as parent visiting day) or parts of the school curriculum that may reactivate your child's grief. In this way, you can be prepared.*

Going forward your child may need language for when people ask about his family. "I have a brother, a mommy, and a daddy, but Daddy died."

Children can be very direct and your child may hear the words, "You don't have a mom!" or something similar in reference to his parent who died. Give him words to respond, such as, "I do have a mom. It's just that she died. She's always with me in my memories."

o   As time passes, talk with your child on occasion about the parent who died so they remain in your child's present life and he knows that mentioning them is not forbidden or taboo.

o   We know that physical objects can represent your missed loved one, but we do not recommend the practice of "enshrining," such as keeping a favorite chair vacant. Instead we encourage keeping aside a small number of your loved one's belongings for you and your child.

o   Sometimes, when you are with your child, your focus must be solely on him, and it is best if you try to put your own needs on hold, difficult as it may be, to tend to his. This will help you both in the long run.

o   Given the demands on you, it is essential to practice self-care—then you can extend that nurturing to your child. Accept help, surround yourself with compassionate adults, and reach out to professionals if necessary to help to ease your pain.

When Your Child's Sibling Has Died

When your own child has died you may be living through what
would be your worst fear. You may be in the depths of despair and
yet you have another child to care for. We offer here some guidance
that we hope will support some of your specific needs and help you
to attend to your surviving child as he comes to terms with the loss
of his sibling.

o   You may struggle with guilt or a sense of failure in not having
    prevented your child's death. This is a common reaction to
    the loss of a child. You may be trying to gain control of the
    situation or attempting to make sure it doesn't happen again.
    Importantly, your mind is working its way through the news,
    processing, and trying to tolerate it.

o   You may be feeling unbearable hopelessness, a physical sort
    of pain that makes you wonder how you'll get through. This
    is your way of taking in your reality, and by being open to
    searing heartbreak you can also open up to happier feelings
    that will eventually last longer and longer over time.

o   Your surviving child's needs may overwhelm you and your
    tolerance level may be low. Checking in with yourself on this
    can give you a reminder to try to be patient with him—and to
    see if you can ask for help from friends and relatives.

o   With everything going on, it is possible that your surviving
    child may not get as much focus as he may need. Try to
    identify figures in his life with whom he feels comfortable and
    whom he can rely on for additional support.

o   The immediacy of this death will become concrete for your
    surviving child quickly as everyday life highlights that his

sibling is not there. Try to stay attuned to this and be present for him or have a trusted grown-up helping you, too.

o Your surviving child may feel additional layers of emotion, including survivor's guilt, as the sibling relationship can be a complicated one.

o Your surviving child may have regrets about things said or done (or not said or done) that cannot be amended now. Let him know that his sibling knew that he loved her and that all brothers and sisters fight and say unkind things sometimes as that happens between people who love each other.

o Your surviving child is likely to be concerned about you and very aware of the extreme sadness you are feeling and may not know how to communicate his needs to you. Be aware that your child:

> *Might feel as if the sibling who died is more special as everyone is so sad that she is no longer alive. Be on the lookout for cues that your child feels this way and let him know often how good it feels to be with him.*

> *Could try to be the perfect child so that you don't have to worry. Let him know that you can handle his worries as well as your own.*

> *May try to gain your attention with "negative" behavior. Try to respond with compassion along with limit-setting rather than reproach.*

o Bear in mind that the death of a young person is fairly rare, which may mean that no one among your surviving child's peers has suffered a similar loss and he may feel more different and alone. If he is open to the idea, you could look into groups or organizations that focus on sibling loss so that he could connect with other children in a similar situation.

o Your child's return to school or childcare will need your careful attention. We provide general guidelines in Chapter 9 and more specific suggestions on pages 203–4. We offer here additional advice to help you to prepare:

> *Talk with teachers about the upcoming school curriculum, as it can include discussions about siblings and the family unit. In this way you and the school can be prepared to support your surviving child.*

o If your surviving child's school is the same one his sibling attended, it may be useful to bear in mind:

> *You may have to create alternative company for him on the journey if he took the bus or traveled to or from school with his sibling.*

> *Your conversations with teachers and other people in the school about your surviving child may be more difficult to navigate as they may all be grieving the death of your child.*

> *Your surviving child's school will not be a "safe haven" as the school community will be affected by the death of his sibling.*

> *Your surviving child may feel he has no escape from grieving, that his private loss has become public. (This heightens the importance of providing spaces for him to be that his sibling was less immersed in, such as a friend's house.)*

> *Teachers, other children, and parents may show heightened discomfort around your surviving child or they may overcompensate by focusing on him in a way that may feel awkward.*

> *Your surviving child may have lost an ally at school now that his sibling is not there.*

Hard realities may be faced every day as he walks past his sibling's locker, homeroom, or friends.

There may be observances and memorials at the school for his sibling that your surviving child may or may not want to attend.

o   Over time, try not to idolize the sibling. Let the memories you share embrace the true fullness of who the sibling was.

o   You may feel the urge to leave the bedroom or personal area of your child who died exactly as it was before the death. We recommend against this but encourage you to keep a few belongings for you and your surviving child.

o   Give your surviving child language to answer questions such as, "How many siblings do you have?" "I have three siblings but one of them died." Or, "Do you have an older sibling?" "Yes, I do, but she died."

o   It is natural to feel an intense hunger to parent after the loss of your child. Be aware that your surviving child might become the repository for all your parenting needs and aspirations, which can lead to an overfocus on him. You might be especially protective of him.

o   You can find solace in recognizing that you are still a parent to your child that died—you are parenting the memory.

When a Close Family Member Has Died by Suicide

If your child's parent, parent figure, or sibling has died by suicide, we can imagine how distraught and confused you may feel right now as you cope with this death. We provide some guidance here with the aim to help you find a way forward for yourself and a path toward supporting your child at this difficult time.

In Chapter 11, we provide the language and a framework for breaking the news to your young child and helping him with his reactions, and we believe it will be helpful for you to read that section. There we suggest that you tell your child that the death was a suicide if he is six or older and give our reasons for doing so. This is not a hard-and-fast rule, and we advise you to pay close attention to your child's needs around this. In essence, we see breaking the news as a two-step process, first giving news of the death, followed by providing the information that it was a suicide at a later time (but before he may hear from others), and we guide you through the telling. We discuss suicide in terms of a disease—suicidality, the result of a tragic loss of hope—which promotes greater compassion and understanding for both you and your child in the moment and as you move forward.

Certain parts of your—and your child's—experience may be intensified and we provide some additional information here in the hope that it may be useful:

o   Your child may feel a multitude of emotions after the death, including guilt. He may believe that he caused his loved one to take her own life and will need to hear very clearly from you, possibly many times over, that he is not to blame in any way for the death. This can be especially true if it is his sibling who has died, as they may have fought or said unkind things to each other beforehand.

o   Your child may have strong feelings of abandonment. Anxiety about the reliability of others may be intensified—especially if it is a parent that has died. Reinforce your connection with your child and demonstrate your own trustworthiness as much as possible. Have other adults in your child's life make efforts to be consistent.

o   Your child may worry that you might end your life. Reassure him with words such as, "I don't have the same sickness and I'm not planning to end my life." Remember though that he will be calmed most by your presence and your attention to his needs and, when you cannot be with him, by the focus and care of other adults in his life.

o   Your child could be concerned that he has the same sickness as his loved one. In the days and weeks following the death, you could tell him that the sickness is not contagious while sending the message that if he is ever feeling hopeless, informing you (or another adult) is the best thing to do. In Chapter 11, we discuss family history of suicide as a risk factor for suicide in a related family member and ways to talk about it with your child.

o   Many people still judge those who die by suicide, and your child is likely to have to navigate other people's opinions. We recommend that you:

   Acknowledge how painful it is to deal with.

   Reiterate to your child that his loved one died because of a disease.

   Explain that not everyone understands (and that some people react harshly to things they don't understand).

Suggest he cannot control what other people say, only his own reaction to it.

Hold tightly to the truth about his loved one's death no matter what others say.

o You will need to work extremely closely with your child's school or childcare to help transition him to the steadying structure of daily activities, and we provide general guidance in Chapter 9 and more specific advice on pages 203–4. Here are additional suggestions:

Your first decision may be whether to mention the cause of death and, in turn, whether to have that information conveyed to teachers, students, and parents. We believe the choice rests with you.

It is likely that the cause of death will become known, especially if it was already publicly mentioned. You may decide that having some control over the narrative may work better for you and your child.

If you decide to have the school provide information about the death, work closely with the administration and the school counselor to develop language that feels right for you and your child to create a letter to the school community.

Let your child know exactly what has been said to teachers and students so that everyone is on the same page.

If classmates ask specifically if the death was a suicide he could respond with, "Yes, my mom ended her own life." "Yes, my sister died by suicide."

Reiterate to your child that he can go to his teacher (or another designated person at the school) anytime he has concerns or needs support.

o   If your child has died by suicide, it is common to feel anxious
     about your surviving child. The idea of keeping him safe may
     be overwhelming. Know that working to build a trusting,
     communicative relationship with him will go a long way
     toward easing your worries.

When You Are Grieving the Loss of an Expected Baby: Miscarriage or Stillbirth

The loss of an expected baby, a sibling to your child, is profoundly painful for everyone in the family and we recommend that you address it with the care for yourself and your child that we have discussed in the rest of the book. Many people—even friends and family—may not understand your grief, may downplay it or say insensitive things, but we suggest that you allow yourself to grieve as you need. Here we provide specific advice for talking with your child:

o   If your baby has died early in your pregnancy and you, or you and your partner, are the only one(s) to know about the pregnancy and the loss, you may think it simpler to say nothing to your child. However, your child will be aware that something is not right within her world and this confusion may lead her to feel anxious and insecure. We suggest that you validate your child's sense that something is different by saying that you are feeling sad. You would add that you (or the person who was pregnant) do not feel well because you have a pain in your belly but you will feel better soon. We think it is hard for children to understand that there was going to be a baby and sadly now there isn't, if there were no significant physical or behavioral changes.

o   If you have shared the news of your pregnancy with others but not your child, she is likely to find out about the loss from overhearing conversations. It is best to let her know that there was going to be a baby, but the pregnancy has ended and a baby won't be born alive. Your child may find this confusing, but you don't really have a choice about telling her, as she would likely find out on her own.

o If you have told your child that you were having a baby, then
   you will need to tell her the sad and difficult news that the
   pregnancy has ended.

o The words you use may depend on how far the pregnancy
   had progressed, how aware your child was that a baby
   was expected and of the role she would play with the baby.
   After the telling, you can explain that the loss is called a
   "miscarriage" or "stillbirth" in case your child hears others
   using the terms. You might say:

   *"We have some sad news. We were going to have a baby, but the
   baby stopped growing and wasn't strong enough to be born. The
   baby died. Let's be together for a while."*

   Or: *"We have something sad to tell you. We told you that we
   were going to have a baby, but sadly the baby couldn't live. The
   baby died. We're all going to spend some time together now."*

   Or: *"We have some sad news to share. Your baby brother was
   not able to be born alive. He died. Let's sit and be together."*

o If the death of the baby necessitates a hospital visit for
   the person who was pregnant, you'll need to let your child
   know, saying something along the lines of: "Mommy is going
   to spend a night in the hospital so that doctors and nurses
   can look after her. Auntie Ada will be here with you, and
   Mommy will be home very soon." You would then take the
   lead from your child, answering questions in simple and
   reassuring ways.

o Be aware that on hearing the news your child may have mixed
   emotions—not every child is only thrilled by the idea of a
   new sibling—and you should accept them without judgment.

o   Your child may believe she is responsible for the death—
    especially if she had negative thoughts about the idea of a
    new baby in the family. Let her know clearly that nothing she
    did or said could have made her baby sibling die.

o   Be aware that your child may feel that the baby is more
    special than she is—so be sure to let her know how happy
    you are to be with her.

o   Let your child's teachers or caregivers know about your loss
    so that they can be supportive of your child, and ask that they
    keep in touch with you to let you know how she is coping.

o   You may want to help your child with language around what
    she could say when asked about the number of siblings she
    has or whether she is an older or younger sibling. Your child
    could say something such as, "I have two sisters. One of them
    died before she was born." "I am an older brother. My baby
    sister died when she was born."

o   We recommend that a ritual take place to commemorate the
    loss and, if news of the pregnancy was public, or if your child
    knew, we recommend involving your child in the planning and
    carrying out.

o   Practice self-care as much as possible, and talk with trusted
    adults, including professionals if necessary, to help to ease
    your pain.

o   The physical side of miscarriage is often overlooked, so be
    sure to acknowledge that your body needs to rest and heal.

o   Allow space for partners who were not pregnant to grieve—
    this is their loss, too.

Our Hopes for You

At this time of heartbreak, you may find that you need to push your emotions down as a way to function, and this can be helpful some of the time, but those feelings still need attention. If you can create small pockets of time in your day to let your feelings emerge (away from your child) and be fully present for them, it will help you more in the long run—though the pain in the here and now can be tremendous.

As you grieve your loved one and support your child through her grief, we hope that you may find moments of relief and solace in speaking with her, that these open conversations feel grounding and hopeful, and that your empathy toward her is reflected back at you.

Chapter 14

There Is
Always Hope . . .
but It May Need to
Be Redefined

✳ Giving Grief Time ✳ Providing a Safe Space for Feelings ✳
✳ Co-existing Emotions ✳ Acknowledging a Loved One at Significant
Events ✳ Unexpected Activators ✳ Tools for Easing Emotions ✳
✳ "Moving Forward With," Rather Than Moving On ✳
✳ Integrating a Death into Ongoing Life ✳ Asynchronous Grieving ✳
✳ Useful Pain ✳ Consulting a Professional ✳
✳ Finding Hope Within Loss ✳

Grief does not fade away and suddenly disappear after a death, and we believe an understanding of this will help parents and their children learn to live with loss. In our work with grieving children and families, we have found that there is no definite timeline for grief, nor is there a prescribed order for passing through different stages—or any stages at all—or a linear movement toward a light at the end of the tunnel. Instead, each person's grief experience is unique. We would say, however, that by allowing your child to grieve at her own pace with your love and support along the way, you will help her through to the other side. There, she will find healing, an ability to remember with less pain the person who died, and the possibility to incorporate those memories into her life story.

Be Prepared to Give Grief the Time and Space You Need

As we described in Chapter 9, there are expectations that your child will grieve in the immediate aftermath of a death, and we provided ways for you to recognize and understand his reactions, and tools to help him with them. Here we hope to support you and your child as you move beyond the first few weeks after the death of someone important to you both, as you learn to absorb the absence of that person into your lives. You may find that there is pressure from others—perhaps even from within—to get on with your life, to accept the loss, to push away your feelings of grief, and to move forward as quickly as possible. Many of us have internalized the notion that grieving for too long is unhealthy, that submerging ourselves in the pain of loss stops us from feeling better. We tell ourselves to have courage, be tough, keep going, and get back to work, to life, so that we don't stop and think about the death because that would pull us down. Often we pass this message on to our children, too, rushing them through grief: "Auntie Sue wouldn't want you to be unhappy still!" or "You need to be brave for your father!" We believe the opposite is true. If you allow yourself and your child to truly grieve over time, to accept the natural grief process, and go through all the emotions that surface, it is possible to make it through, to grow while doing so, and to be restored. Indeed, we would argue that there is value in opening yourself up to the roller coaster of emotions that come with grief and staying with them over time.

Embracing the Grief Process

After telling your child about the death of someone in his world, we have emphasized the importance of:

Validating your child's loss: "I know how much you loved your dog, Buster, and how much you must miss him."

Acknowledging your child's grief: "It looks like you might be feeling mad. Lots of people feel that way when someone they love dies. Would you like a hug?"

Letting your child know that he is seen and that you care: "I know it's been very hard for you since Granny died. There have been many people around and a lot of upset feelings in all of us. I'm here for talking if you want, or we could play a card game."

As your child's life moves beyond the time directly after the death and the rituals that follow, be prepared to continue to validate, acknowledge, and keep him within your sights. You may find that the flurry of activity and influx of well-wishers surrounding a death ebb now, leaving you feeling stranded and alone. This is not unusual as others return to their busy lives, though it may feel like another absence for you in a time already marked by loss. While we know that it is very hard, and the pain you feel is likely to be raw, we suggest that you try not to view this time with yourself and your child as negative. Instead, we advise you to accept the space you have been given to reckon with your new reality as you face the world without someone who meant a great deal to you. Take the time to grieve and allow your emotions, distressing though they may be, to surface so that you can address them. If avoided, ignored, or pushed down these feelings can turn inward and fester. The only way is through. We realize this is a difficult truth, but our experience has shown us that when you acknowledge your hurt and allow yourself to feel the heartache, you can transform it into a useful pain, one that can allow you eventually to have a deeper capacity for love, joy, and empathy.

Take the time to let your child know that it is natural for her grief to last for a while, that she should not be surprised to find her emotions going up and down, or that she is experiencing a lot of different emotions, and encourage her to continue to express her feelings as she needs. For some children, the absence of a person builds up over time and the realization of the permanence of death can hit them, suddenly and hard, some time after the actual death occurred. Children can hold themselves together for weeks or months, and then appear to feel intense emotions and react to the death belatedly. When this happens, parents and teachers may consider such grieving as a step backward, as inappropriate, instead of a way that grief can occur in anyone, and they send the message that the child's behavior needs to change just when she needs their support and understanding the most. Some children who lose someone close to them feel the need to hide their grief away, suppressing their emotions, because they want to fit in at school, or they don't want to burden others with their problems. The more you can be aware, as a parent, of the ways in which—and when—grief may show itself, or be pushed below the surface, the more you can let your child know that she has a safe space with you for sharing her feelings for as long as she needs.

As Life Moves Forward, Grief May Continue

Recently, a friend of Elena's called to talk about her sister-in-law who had died four months earlier, leaving behind her nine- and eleven-year-old niece and nephew. Through tears, she said, "I'm still having a very hard time and really struggling with this but Lucy and George are fine! I think they've had as much closure as possible. They go to school, they have friends, I see them laughing . . . so I think they are really okay. Right, Elena?"

Our response is that processing takes place over years, not only at the time that someone dies. It is true that children are resilient and they can still thrive after a powerful loss, but that doesn't mean that they are "fine." Just as Elena's friend, who was managing to go to work every day and make dinner for her family each night, was not fine. Our minds automatically help to dose out the pain so some measure of this "seeming fine" is adaptive, but it is likely that Lucy's and George's hearts were still aching and that they missed their mother every day even while continuing their daily activities.

TAKEAWAY

The ache of loss can co-exist with the ability to laugh.

Elena responded to her friend's question by saying it was terrific that Lucy and George were able to engage in their lives, while adding that they might be struggling at times, too. "Do you ever talk about their mom with them? Even if it makes you a bit tearful?" Elena asked. "It could be helpful to do so once in a while when natural cues arise, and if they feel sadness as you refer to her, it might allow them to express it. And if not, you have at least opened the door for talking."

We find it is helpful for you to continue to model for your child throughout your grieving and let him see your own sorrow or

confusion, when you are in control of it, to articulate that expressing such feelings is a good thing. You can show smiles and laughter,
too, when you are able, demonstrating that we all feel a full range
of emotions when we are grieving, often within the same day. Remember that your child may
feel emotions such as anger,
fear, guilt, bitterness, relief,
and shame as part of grieving and should be given the
opportunity to communicate
them without judgment. Many
children are surprised that

TAKEAWAY
We can feel all the emotions
of grieving even as we
embrace life as it is without
the loved one.

they have emotions other than sadness after a death and often need
permission to show them. We also recommend that you go one step
further and state directly to your child that it is okay to *not* have
particular thoughts and feelings, but when he does, it is helpful to
express them.

If the person who died was significant in your child's life, we recommend keeping a photograph or two in a visible place, so your
child sees that the person is remembered and not hidden away. You
could bring them into conversations, "Do you remember how Nata-
lie loved banana bread?" as you enjoy the baked treat together, so
that your child knows it is okay to talk about the person. In this way,
she sees that the person lives on in memories and is still connected
to events in her own life.

Handling the Emotional Pain of Significant Events

Jenna had mixed feelings on her ninth birthday. Her mom had gone
out of her way to plan the perfect day with a homemade chocolate
cake, and a party with her family and Jenna's best friend, Viola. But
Jenna just wanted her dad to be there. He'd died in a car accident

ten months earlier and she missed him. She didn't want to upset her mom so she sat at the table and opened presents and smiled at the guests. But when the candles on her cake were lit and everyone was singing "Happy Birthday," she just couldn't stop the tears from running down her face. She sank into her chair, sobbing. She was sure she had ruined the party. Next she felt her mom's soft hands rubbing her shoulders. "It's okay, Jenna," she said. "I miss Dad, too. I wish he were here with us." Her mom's voice shook. "He loved birthday parties," added Grandma Ellen quietly. "Sang so loudly," said Grandpa Jack, "and out of tune, too!" Jenna looked up as everyone at the party remembered her dad and said something they had liked about him. Her mom was crying now and laughing, too, and that's how Jenna felt, sad and happy at the same time. Watching her mom, she realized it was okay to still feel sad, that it was natural to miss her dad because she'd loved him so much, and that she could still be happy even though he wasn't with her anymore.

Jenna's mother told Michael this story at her monthly check-in—she had started to meet with him after her husband's sudden death and found it useful to talk about her own grief and Jenna's, too. "It sounds like you handled the situation very well," said Michael. "You let Jenna know it's okay to have fun even while she's missing her dad. She's human and we have complicated feelings."

"Do you think Jenna should come and see you?"

"I think you're both communicating about her feelings really well. She is able to be sad sometimes and happy sometimes, and so I don't think she needs to. But let's keep an eye on it."

Many people feel guilty about laughing after someone has died, even dismayed to find that they still have any capacity for pleasure. They may wonder if there is something wrong with them, if it means that they have forgotten about their loved one. It's important to let your child know—especially as children dose their grief, and play is so crucial to that process—that joy does not negate the sadness she feels about the loss of a loved one, that the feelings can exist together. It can also be helpful for children to understand that their sorrow will not last forever.

Grief is a process and it happens over time. It can come in waves. It may retreat and return, stronger than before, then recede again. As Jenna was learning, certain times of year can be especially painful, such as holidays and birthdays, as can family events at which the loved one would have been present. Many people experience a resurgence of grief as the death date approaches each year. We recommend that you plan to acknowledge the loss at these times, and that a ritual—which could be very brief if that feels best—is observed. In this way, you have some measure of directing the feelings that are likely to bubble up and you can give them a place to go. When you talk with your child about grief, it can be helpful to say something such as, "Everyone feels different things as they grieve and sometimes a lot of those feelings can show up at certain times. That might happen on days such as your birthday or on your brother's birthday."

We recommend that you involve your child in the planning and carrying out of rituals. On a loved one's birthday, you might light a candle, buy flowers, release a balloon in their memory, or visit their grave. At a graduation, someone might say a sentence, "We're remembering Dad today and wishing that he were here celebrating with us." It may seem terribly painful to talk about someone who has died, and the inclination may be to avoid doing so, but this is useful pain. By addressing the hurt and the loss directly, you give feelings that are already present a way to be expressed and not stifled, and the shared moment can help to ease the heartache. By giving the emotions a time and place to be felt, by allowing yourself to acknowledge them, you are freeing yourself—and your child—to engage more wholeheartedly in the special day. By remembering someone out loud, you also convey to your child that while a loved one may

have died they are not forgotten; their story continues.
Jenna's mother or another
adult might have said something simple at the beginning
of her birthday party, such as,
"Jenna, your dad loved celebrating your birthday and we

TAKEAWAY

Have a time and space
during celebrations and
holidays to remember a
missed loved one.

---

wish he were here with us." Such a statement may have helped Jenna
to know from the start that it was okay to remember her father and
to realize that wishing he were there would not ruin the party. Instead, she tried to bury her emotions until they burst out of her—at
which point her family was able to support her beautifully.

Unexpected Activators—Facing the Emotions

It is helpful for you and your child to be aware that unexpected activators can bring on memories and waves of grief, even long after
the initial loss: hearing music that was playing when you learned
about your loved one's death, a waft of perfume, an ambulance's
siren, or perhaps thinking that you see your loved one on the street.
Sometimes it is these unanticipated reminders that will hit you or
your child the hardest because of the surprise element and the way
grief is tapped into without plan or warning. One way to cope with
the inevitability of these moments is to offer your child the inner
resources to manage the feelings as they arise instead of pushing
them away or shutting down in the face of them. We recommend
that you model with your child how to welcome the feeling, name
it, and handle it. It is a way of walking through the pain in a productive manner to emerge on the other side, more resilient and ready to
continue to engage with life.

For example, if you're in a store with your child and Gran's favorite
music comes on, catching you unaware, and your child notices you

tearing up, you might say, "That music made me think of Gran. I wasn't expecting it and it made me feel sad. I'm taking some deep breaths to let me focus on where we are now and that helps me feel better."

To clarify, we are not advising you share your grief with your child every time you react to a reminder of your loss. The idea is not to lay your grief on him. Instead, if your child sees you express your emotions brought on by an unanticipated memory, we recommend that you be honest about the reason for your distress, say that it is natural to be affected, and let him know how you cope.

If, in a similar scenario, you notice your child seems suddenly sad or is showing strong emotions in response to something, you can help her through the feeling.

"It looks like you might be feeling mad about those kids playing soccer. Did something upset you?" You may be thinking that your child loved kicking the ball around with her uncle who died recently and she could be remembering that and missing him. Instead of suggesting that to your child when she has made no reference to him, you could offer her a way to move through the anger, such as running or jumping. "Want to run around a bit to help the mad run through your body?"

In this way, your child learns coping mechanisms and when she feels sudden and powerful emotions of grief, she can say, "I know that feeling, and this is how I deal with it." You might teach your child the words, "If I can feel it, I can deal with it, and heal."

Here are some activities for facing and easing intense feelings:

o   Deep breathing

o   Playing music

o   Singing

o   Squeezing a stress ball

o Running, jumping, playing

o Mindfulness and meditation (we offer some examples in Resources)

As you help your child to navigate grief, you have many opportunities to support and guide her and help her strengthen and grow. However, there are going to be moments when she is overwhelmed and when, despite your best efforts, she throws a tantrum in public or says something hurtful to you. Or she might withdraw into herself or break down in tears, perhaps leading you to feel helpless and unhelpful. The best advice we can offer in these situations is to try to be patient and compassionate with your child, to be kind to yourself, and to remember that tomorrow is another day.

"Moving Forward With," Rather Than Moving On

We discourage use of the phrase and concept of "moving on" after a death because people don't leave a death behind. We believe the path to healing, to engaging joyfully in life after a loss, is by incorporating that loss into the fabric of your sense of yourself and your life story. By *moving forward with* the loss. A death will shape the rest of your—and your child's—life in painful, and even positive, ways. Your child may need to process his understanding of a death many times as he matures and he sees the way his life and his sense of self are directly affected by loss. We have emphasized throughout the book the importance of returning to conversations about the death of a loved one after the initial breaking of the news, and we repeat that here. A three-year-old will need to address a loss many times over as he grows older

> **TAKEAWAY**
> We do not move on; we move forward with a loss as part of who we are.

and his comprehension of death in general and his specific loss in particular deepens. As you revisit past conversations with him and answer questions old and new, he will meld this latest knowledge into his previous understanding and sort through what it means to him now.

In past chapters, we have talked about your child needing a six-year-old version of breaking the news and an eight-year-old version and a twelve-year-old version and on into his teens. Each time there may be new elements about the death itself that he may understand more fully (or that you are able to share with him), and he himself may take the information on board differently because he has passed through another developmental stage. As your child matures, his capacity to understand who he was at the time of the loss and his relationship to the person who died expands and deepens. A twelve-year-old may suddenly realize that he need not feel ashamed about quitting baseball at the age of nine, after his uncle died. Now that he has matured he may be able to see his turning away from the game as the act of an overwhelmed and desperately sad younger version of himself, not that of a quitter.

As your child grows older, you can support her as she refines the story she carries within her and integrates the death into her ongoing life. A child who is upset that she can't invite her grandfather to Grandparents Day can be helped to see that she has two great-uncles and a neighbor who would love to accompany her. Often it's a matter of reframing the issue and focusing on what is still possible rather than only on what is no longer possible—you allow for both.

Sometimes children are forced to reckon with who they are in the wake of a death by a peer's thoughtless observation: "You don't have a grandma!" This is one of those unexpected moments that sets off intense pain and grief. It also brings with it the realization for your child (and for you) that others may view her in a different way now, that she is marked by loss. You can help your child by providing her with language to use in these situations, but also to reassure her when troubling questions arise within. "I still have a grandma. She's always with me in my memory." Let her know that she will always have a grandpa or mother or brother and will always have a connection to them even though they have died. "She is always with you in the love she gave you and that you showed her. Nothing can take that away."

Asynchronous Grieving

Sometimes your child's need to reassess or reprocess a death may feel at odds with your own needs. As he is developing and expanding his cognitive and emotional faculties more so than you, he may have ongoing questions at a time when you would prefer not to dive into the details of a death again. Or there may be days when you may be feeling hopeful about the future and your child's questions or emotions may seem discordant. We might refer to this as asynchronous grieving. This can often occur as no two people grieve in the same way or on the same timeline, and it is true for you, your child, and any member of your family or friend circle. We have encouraged you throughout the book to be available for your child's questions and to respond with honesty and empathy, and yet we understand that there are times when this is just not possible, perhaps never more so than when you are coming to terms with the loss of a loved one yourself. Maybe you are overwhelmed or exhausted or pressed for time.

What you can show your child at such a time is that it is important for everyone to respect the grieving process of other people. If you feel you cannot handle a conversation that taps into your pain over the loss at the moment when your child asks, you can offer an answer such as, "How about if we talk about this after lunch when I can sit down with you and concentrate on it?" Or you could suggest that he talk with another particular adult (whom you know is willing and available) about it if he wishes to discuss it right away. "What if you ask Aunt Bess that question this time, as I think she could answer it better."

One of Elena's patients felt he was growing apart from his young daughter as he was avoiding spending time in the car alone with her. In the past, father and daughter would chat during car rides, but in recent months the girl had started to ask questions about cancer whenever they were together in the car. Her mother had died of lung cancer the year before and while the father had been open about the death and had many conversations about it with his daughter, sometimes he felt the need to put it aside.

As Elena listened, she was able to empathize with her patient's need to lessen his pain while helping him to see that his daughter was seeking connection with him, and perhaps a way of remembering her mother, or coping with anxious feelings, through talking about cancer. Together he and Elena were able to come up with strategies that enabled him to create space for conversations with his daughter at times when he felt emotionally prepared for them, when he could invite her questions. He realized that he had been avoiding the topic and his daughter had seen the car rides as an opportunity to talk when he was unable to escape. With Elena's guidance, he purchased an age-appropriate book on cancer so that he and his daughter could look through it and have conversations together. As he made himself available to her and her questions, on terms that worked for him as well as her, he noticed that the car ride questions about cancer diminished. But when they did arise he felt more able to say, "Let's talk about that when I can focus on it better," and to suggest a time to sit together and have a conversation.

Useful or Productive Pain

We have talked about the term "useful pain" or "productive pain" as a way to help you to understand the value of opening yourself up—and encouraging your child to do the same—to difficult emotions while grieving. We believe that when the multitude of feelings brought up by grief are faced and felt, they move through us and become less disturbing over time.

Avoiding feelings of sadness comes with a cost, as it is impossible to shut down our capacity to experience sorrow without cutting off our access to other emotions, including happier ones. In our work, we have seen unprocessed grief turn inward, causing struggles for people as they try to move forward with their lives. It can manifest as fear of intimacy, as a reluctance to experience love, and in the development of stunted relationships. For your child to be able to find her capacity for a full range of emotions again, it is important for her to process sadness and the many other feelings she may be experiencing. If you facilitate her grieving fully, she will enhance her ability to ultimately flourish.

One of Michael's patients, nine-year-old Ruby, was having a difficult time coping with her father's death. She hadn't wanted to talk about it with her mother directly after it happened, putting her hands over her ears or leaving a room if she ever mentioned it, and in the weeks that followed she often became angry. Though she was attending school as usual, she had stopped spending time with friends, preferring to watch TV alone. After a couple of months, Ruby's mother brought her to see Michael for help. Following his initial session with Ruby, Michael wanted to ensure that he respected the young girl's natural grief response of cycles of silence and anger—a potential way of dosing—while making sure that Ruby was not shutting down her emotions in a way that would limit healing. As Michael and Ruby continued to meet, it became clear that her feelings of rage were not being managed in productive ways that could help her. She was stifling her grief and avoiding it until the anger had nowhere else to go. When it burst out of her in a fury she would yell at her mom and then shut it down by playing video games. "My mom doesn't like it when I'm mad," she said.

Michael helped Ruby and her mother to see that Ruby's anger was a natural response to her father's death and that instead of trying to make it go away when it arose, she could allow it, feel it, and manage it. Over the next few weeks, Ruby learned to recognize the waves of emotion as they rushed through her body. "I feel like an anger monster," she said to her mom. In the past, she would have yelled and then pushed the anger down and distracted herself with video games, but now she was beginning to learn to throw beanbags into a hoop, to let the anger ripple through her. It was a start.

When to Consult a Professional

Since the grief process can continue for many months and is different for everyone, it may be hard to know if and when to consult a professional about how your child is doing. You could certainly talk with a professional at any time if you think your child might benefit, but we would say that if your child's grief is getting in the way of her usual functioning four to six weeks after the death of a loved one, then it is time to consult with a professional about your concerns. This could include: your pediatrician, your child's teacher, a school counselor, a mental health professional, or a member of your religious institution. We want to be sure to emphasize that it is natural for your child to be grieving still at six weeks—it is just when grief stops a child from carrying out her usual daily tasks, responsibilities, and social activities that we advise a consultation with a professional.

Finding Hope Within Loss

During sad and frightening times, it is often hard to imagine much that is positive or to look ahead optimistically. We are here to tell you that within every painful situation, even after the death of a loved one, there are things to be hopeful about. It might be that feelings do get easier over time. Or it could be as simple as the fact that your child will have a play date next week and that there will be other fun events in the future to look toward. It can be hopeful to find meaning in the loss and it can be important to show this to your child. If she has made a video sending love to her teacher who is dying, or she has painted a picture for her grieving grandpa, you can highlight for her that out of the pain she has done something good and kind. She has made a difference in someone else's life, a powerful thought. Some people find meaning in their grief by channeling their energy to help ensure that the kind of loss they have experienced does not happen to other people or to help those who have been through it—by raising money for research into a disease or volunteering at an organization the loved one believed in. The underlying message you can give to your child when you find positives in the negative is that life is filled with different and sometimes seemingly conflicting emotions. That this duality is natural and can be embraced as part of being human. When you find uplifting thoughts, feelings, or actions amid emotional pain, you are paving the way not for moving on, but rather for "moving forward with" this loss as part of your story and your child's story.

Devastating though a loss can be, we believe that if you are open and together with your child in the face of it, are able to talk and embrace its impact, then your lives can be deepened by it as you move forward.

Just four weeks after her younger daughter's death, Elena spent Thanksgiving with her family and their close relatives. It was a really difficult time for everyone. One particular afternoon, after making a salad with her sister-in-law, Elena sat alone in the living room, deep in sadness. The three children—Elena's older daughter, Molly, and her two older cousins—were upstairs. Elena could hear them giggling and through her sorrow she was glad that Molly was able to enjoy herself. Suddenly the girls came bounding downstairs in grown-up clothes snagged from their parents' belongings, even a sequined top hat, and ran into the living room, fizzing with excitement. They'd been working on a play for the adults and now as Elena watched their performance with her husband, sister-in-law, and brother-in-law she was astonished to find that she could feel pleasure. She sat, recognizing Molly's courage and resilience, the love that had gone into the girls' show as they hoped to ease the adults' pain. She realized that her heart was able to open to other feelings than agony amid her grief. And while she knew it wouldn't last, this glimmer was a precious hint that her capacity for joy and for feeling the love offered by others might one day return. It was a revelatory and transformative moment.

We believe this is possible for you and your child as well. Embracing grief can bring renewed appreciation for the everyday or small things in life, and build a deeper capacity for love and pleasure, and a different sense of purpose.

RESOURCES

We compiled this selection of resources to offer you further tools to help you find your path forward. The information we give here has proved useful to our patients and to us, and we hope it may give you additional guidance.

We include:
- A list of helpful organizations and their websites
- Recommended reading (both children's books and adult books)
- Techniques for coping with emotions, such as breathing exercises and mindfulness and meditation for children

ORGANIZATIONS HELPING GRIEVING FAMILIES

Bereaved Parents of the USA (bereavedparentsusa.org) helps parents and families to navigate grief after the death of a child.

The Coalition to Support Grieving Students (grievingstudents.org) is a collaboration of organizations representing school professionals who strongly believe that bereaved students need the support of their school community. Informed by the expertise of leading bereavement expert Dr. David Schonfeld, it provides many free resources on how to help grieving children.

The Compassionate Friends (compassionatefriends.org) supports families after the death of a child.

COPE (copefoundation.org) is a nonprofit grief and healing organization dedicated to helping parents and families living with the loss of a child. It offers support groups and workshops and, as part of the Eluna Network (see below), organizes Camp Erin for grieving children.

Courageous Parents Network (courageousparentsnetwork.org) orients, empowers, and accompanies families caring for children with serious illness.

The Dougy Center (dougy.org) offers extensive online grief resources and support and a safe place to connect before and after a death.

Eluna Network (elunanetwork.org) helps children and families impacted by grief and addiction through multiple programs and an online resources library. It also offers bereavement support for children through Camp Erin and addiction prevention and mentoring for children with Camp Mariposa. Camps are offered throughout the United States free of charge.

First Candle/SIDS Alliance (firstcandle.org) offers resources including a 24/7 crisis hotline for grieving families after sleep-related infant deaths.

Grief (grief.com) was founded by David Kessler, an expert on grief and loss, and the website is filled with practical resources and information, including on support groups and grief counselors.

GriefShare (griefshare.org) offers free support groups and seminars for people who are grieving.

MISS Foundation (missfoundation.org) provides education and support to families grieving the death of a child, including through support groups, online forums, and workshops.

The National Alliance for Children's Grief (childrengrieve.org) raises awareness about the needs of children and teens who are grieving a death, and provides education and resources for anyone who supports them.

Reimagine (letsreimagine.org) is a nonprofit organization that draws on the arts, design, medicine, and spirituality to transform cultural attitudes around death and grief.

Sesame Street in Communities (sesamestreetincommunities.org /topics/grief/) provides activities, videos, and articles to help children understand and process grief.

ORGANIZATIONS RELATED TO SUICIDE

Suicide Loss

Alliance of Hope (allianceofhope.org) provides support and resources to suicide loss survivors.

SAVE (save.org) serves as a resource to those touched by suicide as well as aiming to prevent suicide through public awareness.

Hotlines

Crisis Text Line (crisistextline.org)
    Text HOME to 741741 to connect.

National Suicide Prevention Lifeline (suicidepreventionlifeline.org)
    This is a 24-hour crisis line:
    1-800-273-TALK (8255).

Information and Prevention

American Foundation for Suicide Prevention (afsp.org) provides information and help to prevent suicide and support to those in crisis or touched by suicide.

JED Foundation (jedfoundation.org) aims to protect emotional health and prevent suicide in teens and young adults.

Rethink the Conversation (rethinktheconversation.org) aims to shift perspective around suicide, and advocates for open conversations, especially around bullying and suicide.

Seize the Awkward (seizetheawkward.org) helps to navigate difficult conversations about mental health and suicide.

The Trevor Project (thetrevorproject.org) offers crisis intervention and suicide prevention services for LGBTQ youth.

U.S. Department of Veterans Affairs Mental Health (mentalhealth.va.gov /suicide_prevention/index.asp) aims to prevent suicide among veterans.

SUPPORT FOR PARENTS EXPERIENCING MISCARRIAGE OR STILLBIRTH LOSS

Empty Arms Bereavement Support (emptyarmsbereavement.org) provides resources to help families through miscarriage, stillbirth, and infant loss.

Now I Lay Me Down to Sleep (nowilaymedowntosleep.org) provides remembrance portraits to families that have experienced the death of a baby. A network of volunteer photographers in the United States and twenty-five international countries offers compassionate bereavement photography services, allowing families to honor their babies and their short lives.

Perinatal Hospice (perinatalhospice.org) offers resources for caring perinatal hospice support when a baby is given a fatal diagnosis during pregnancy.

Still Standing Magazine (stillstandingmag.com) was founded in 2012 and supports those struggling with child loss—from conception to adulthood.

CREATING AN ONLINE MEMORIAL PAGE FOR YOUR LOVED ONE

There are many options for setting up an online memorial for your loved one with photos, stories, and tributes to keep memories alive. We list some of the more popular ones here. All of these are free but be aware that there may be charges for more complex pages. Some of these sites offer supportive and practical information around loss, but we list them here for the purpose of providing an option for you to create a memorial.
forevermissed.com
gatheringus.com
memories.net
mykeeper.com

BOOKS FOR YOUNG CHILDREN

Understanding Death

The Fall of Freddie the Leaf by Leo Buscaglia

Freddie the leaf cycles through spring and summer, enjoying his time with fellow leaves and guided by a wise friend. As fall arrives and leaves around him tumble down, he becomes aware that everything dies, including himself. A good introduction to the concept of death, though be aware that Freddie's death is described as falling asleep—which we do not recommend. Appealing nature photographs illustrate the story.

Lifetimes by Bryan Mellonie, illustrated by Robert Ingpen

Talks about life cycles in plants, animals, and people and reminds us that dying is part of life.

What Happens When a Loved One Dies by Dr. Jillian Roberts, illustrated by Cindy Revell

Three children ask simple questions about dying, and honest answers touch on human death, funerals, the afterlife, and grief. An excellent book for starting conversations. Bright, child-friendly illustrations complement the text.

When Dinosaurs Die: A Guide to Understanding Death by Laurie Krasny Brown and Marc Brown

A thorough look at death and grief through the eyes of a likable community of dinosaurs. Includes explanations about different causes of death (touching on suicide, war, drug abuse), what death means, feelings, after-death customs, and ways to remember a loved one. Busy illustrations engage the reader and encourage discussions.

Death of Loved Ones

After a Death: An Activity Book for Children by Amy Barrett Lindholm
(The Dougy Center)

A workbook for children who have experienced the death of someone
in their lives. Includes drawing and writing activities to remember their
loved one and learn ways to live with their loss.

Ben's Flying Flowers by Inger Maier, illustrated by Maria Bogade

When her younger brother Ben dies after a long illness, Emily withdraws
from her life, stating, "I'm never drawing happy pictures again." Over
time, with the support of her parents, she finds ways to manage her
sadness and to move forward with memories of Ben. Simple illustrations
capture Emily's emotions.

Death Is Stupid by Anastasia Higginbotham

Written through the eyes of a child grappling with confusion, sadness,
and anger after the death of a beloved grandmother, this frank yet
sensitive picture book validates a child's emotions while asking difficult
questions. Open, truthful, and funny, it does an excellent job of looking
at death from a child's perspective. Illustrated with striking collages.

Everett Anderson's Goodbye by Lucille Clifton, illustrated
by Ann Grifalconi

Portrays a young boy's experiences of grief after his father's death.
While we do not adhere to the concept of stages of grief or the idea that
grief is linear, this book shows a child's many feelings after a death in a
thoughtful, compassionate way. Soft black-and-white drawings beautifully
reveal the boy's emotions.

Ida, Always by Caron Levis, illustrated by Charles Santoso

Inspired by polar bears that lived in New York City's Central Park Zoo,
this tender story explores friendship, terminal illness, and loss. On
learning that Ida is sick, Gus is devastated, and together the friends

navigate anger, sadness, and love as they share her last days. Thoughtful, compassionate, and ultimately hopeful—with rich illustrations that portray the bears' emotional journey.

The Invisible String by Patrice Karst, illustrated by Joanne Lew-Vriethoff

A mother explains to her children that an invisible string made of love connects everyone who loves one another so they need never feel alone. One line alludes to separation after death and the concept can help children understand that love and memories can last forever. The word "heaven" could be changed to reflect other spiritual beliefs.

The Memory Box: A Book About Grief by Joanna Rowland, illustrated by Thea Baker

A young girl worries about forgetting her loved one and finds that talking about memories, making a memory box, and creating new memories all help her to navigate the loss. Illustrations filled with detailed patterns add a hopeful feel.

One Wave at a Time: A Story About Grief and Healing by Holly Thompson, illustrated by Ashley Crowley

After the death of his father, Kai experiences waves of feelings "as unpredictable as the sea" as he and his family adjust to their new life. A sensitive, helpful, and realistic look at the many shapes of grief and ways to move forward with memories of a loved one. Striking illustrations are both delicate and bold and capture the many waves of emotions.

The Scar by Charlotte Moundlic, illustrated by Olivier Tallec

A young boy navigates the painful reality of his mother's death, his father's grief, and his own roller-coaster ride of emotions as he worries about forgetting his mother. Beautifully written, honest, tender, and ultimately reassuring with poignant illustrations.

When Someone Dies: A Child-Caregiver Activity Book
by the National Alliance for Grieving Children

An activity book for children to help them express, understand, and cope with their grief. Each page also offers guidance for adults to connect with their child on the subjects of death, dying, and bereavement.

Death of a Pet

The Day Tiger Rose Said Goodbye by Jane Yolen, illustrated by Jim LaMarche

Written from the point of view of Tiger Rose, a cat whose "kitten days [are] so long ago," this lyrical story follows her final day as she says goodbye, then curls up under rosebushes and leaves "her old and tired body behind." Moving and wise with soft, realistic illustrations.

Sammy in the Sky by Barbara Walsh, illustrated by Jamie Wyeth

The book's narrator and her hound dog, Sammy, are inseparable, spending endless days and nights together. When Sammy gets sick and dies, the girl misses her best friend—until one day she spots him in the sky and realizes he is still with her. Stunning realistic full-page paintings capture the special bond between a child and her pet.

When a Pet Dies by Fred Rogers, photographs by Jim Judkis

A reassuring, straightforward explanation about the death of a pet and feelings that might arise, written by the beloved TV host. Emphasizes the importance of talking about emotions. Simple (though dated) photographs document several children's journeys through grief.

Books About Feelings

Angry Arthur by Hiawyn Oram, illustrated by Satoshi Kitamura

A young boy is so angry that he imagines destroying the world but learns the valuable lesson that his thoughts have caused no harm. This book gives children ways to name the emotion "angry" and to learn what it looks like.

The Boy, the Mole, the Fox and the Horse by Charlie Mackesy

A book for all ages. The characters share their fears and hopes about kindness, friendship, and love, tenderly illustrated with delightful color and black-and-white drawings.

Each Kindness by Jacqueline Woodson, illustrated by E. B. Lewis

When a new girl comes to school, Chloe is unkind to her. The girl keeps trying to make friends and Chloe continues to be unkind—until the day the girl doesn't come back and Chloe is left to think about her actions. Shows the value of kindness and empathy. Beautiful watercolors draw the reader into each page.

Grumpy Monkey by Suzanne Lang, illustrated by Max Lang

Jim Panzee is grumpy—though it takes a while for him to acknowledge that it's true. His friends try to get him to change his mood and, after storming away from them, Jim realizes it's okay to be grumpy and that the feeling will pass. You and your child could brainstorm ways that Jim could feel mad without upsetting his friends. Fun cartoony watercolors throughout.

I Am Enough by Grace Byers, illustrated by Keturah A. Bobo

A celebration of all that young girls can be—by believing in their own self-worth. Lyrical verse encourages self-confidence and kindness to oneself and others while bright illustrations depict girls of diverse skin colors and body types.

In My Heart: A Book of Feelings by Jo Witek, illustrated by Christine Roussey

"My heart is full of feelings. Big feelings and small feelings. Loud feelings and quiet feelings. Quick feelings and slow feelings. My heart is like a house, with all these feelings living inside." Names and describes different emotions. Vivid, mischievous illustrations.

The Most Magnificent Thing by Ashley Spires

A girl struggles to create a magnificent thing and becomes frustrated and angry—until her dog suggests she take a walk. Spare, humorous illustrations portray the girl's emotions and those of her loyal dog, too.

The Rabbit Listened by Cori Doerrfeld

Taylor is proud when he builds something amazing . . . but then it comes crashing down. All his animal friends step in to fix his problem but Taylor doesn't feel like following their suggestions. In the end a rabbit arrives, sits with Taylor, and listens. Sometimes that is exactly what is needed. Sweet, evocative illustrations capture Taylor's shifting moods.

When Sadness Is at Your Door by Eva Eland

Sadness is portrayed as an unexpected visitor in this reassuring book, arriving at the door with a suitcase. Instead of pushing the newcomer away, a young girl listens and tries to find out what it needs. Together she and Sadness try calming activities like drawing, listening to music, and walking in the woods. Helpful and practical with gentle, spare illustrations.

BOOKS FOR OLDER CHILDREN

Healing Your Grieving Heart for Teens: 100 Practical Ideas by Alan D. Wolfelt

This offers ideas for activities that help a teen cope with loss and teaches that grief thoughts and feelings are important to experience.

I Will Remember You: A Guidebook Through Grief for Teens by Laura Dower and Elena Lister

A book for a teen to read on their own if they suffer a loss. They will learn how other teens have coped and will find useful activities in music, art, and writing to help them process their grief. Includes a resources section.

Remembering Mrs. Rossi by Amy Hest, illustrated by Heather Maione

Eight-year-old Annie misses her mother, a sixth-grade teacher, who died suddenly the summer before. As she and her father try to come to terms with the loss, she finds hope in a book of memories written by her mother's students. Thoughtful, humorous, and real. Sensitive black-and-white illustrations throughout.

The Thing About Jellyfish by Ali Benjamin

When her friend drowns, Suzy is convinced that a jellyfish sting caused the death and in her grief she throws herself into proving her theory. Her single-minded—and silent—focus isolates her from friends and family until she realizes that the support she has needed has been there all along. Told with emotional insight and compassion.

BOOKS FOR ADULTS

Books About Dying, Death, and End of Life

The Art of Dying Well: A Practical Guide to a Good End of Life by Katy Butler

A Beginner's Guide to the End: Practical Advice for Living Life and Facing Death by B. J. Miller and Shoshana Berger

Being Mortal by Atul Gawande

The Best Care Possible and *Dying Well* by Ira Byock

The Conversation: A Revolutionary Plan for End-of-Life Care by Angelo E. Volandes

Extreme Measures: Finding a Better Path to the End of Life by Jessica Nutik Zitter

The Five Invitations: Discovering What Death Can Teach Us About Living Fully by Frank Ostaseski

How We Die: Reflections on Life's Final Chapter by Sherwin Nuland

The Lost Art of Dying: Reviving Forgotten Wisdom by L. S. Dugdale

When Breath Becomes Air by Paul Kalanithi

Books on Feelings and Grief

35 Ways to Help a Grieving Child by the Dougy Center staff

The AfterGrief: Finding Your Way Along the Long Arc of Loss and *Motherless Daughters* by Hope Edelman

Anxiety: The Missing Stage of Grief by Claire Bidwell Smith

The Anxious Parent by Michael Schwartzman

Bearing the Unbearable: Love, Loss, and the Heartbreaking Path of Grief by Joanne Cacciatore

The Choice: Embrace the Possible and *The Gift: 12 Lessons to Save Your Life* by Edith Eger

The Death of a Child: Reflections for Grieving Parents by Elaine E. Stillwell

Finding Meaning: The Sixth Stage of Grief by David Kessler

The Gifts of Imperfection and *Rising Strong* by Brené Brown

Giving a Voice to Sorrow by Steve Zeitlin and Ilana Harlow (includes a chapter by Elena Lister)

Grief Day by Day: Simple Practices and Daily Guidance for Living with Loss by Jan Warner

The Grieving Student: A Guide for Schools by David Schonfeld and Marcia Quackenbush

Healing After Loss: Daily Meditations for Working Through Grief by Martha Whitmore Hickman

Healing Your Grieving Heart: 100 Practical Ideas by Alan Wolfelt

I Wasn't Ready to Say Goodbye: Surviving, Coping, and Healing After the Sudden Death of a Loved One by Brook Noel and Pamela Blair

In the Midst of Winter: Selections from the Literature of Mourning edited by Mary Jane Moffat

It's OK That You're Not OK by Megan Devine

The Other Side of Sadness: What the New Science of Bereavement Tells Us About Life After Loss by George Bonnano

When Children Grieve: For Adults to Help Children Deal with Death, Divorce, Pet Loss, Moving, and Other Losses by John W. James, Russell Friedman, and Leslie Matthews

Books on Mindfulness

Calm and Peaceful, Mindful Me by Andrea Dorn

The Mindful Child and *Mindful Games* by Susan Kaiser Greenland

The Mindful Family by Renda Dionne Madrigal

Mindfulness for Kids Who Worry by Katie Austin

The Mindfulness Journal for Kids by Hannah Sherman

TECHNIQUES FOR COPING WITH EMOTIONS

Breathing Exercises for Your Child

Getting Started

- o With a hand on the belly, breathe in through the nose for a count of ten and feel the belly fill with air and then breathe out through the mouth for ten.

- o You can ask your child to imagine they are breathing in a calming color and picture it filling their belly before they breathe it out.

- o Lying down with a stuffed animal on the belly, take a deep breath in and out and watch the animal move up and down.

- o Have your child imagine he has a wand to blow bubbles in his hand. Take a deep breath in through his nose and then slowly breathe out through his mouth as if he is trying to blow a great big bubble through the wand. Imagine the bubble blowing away and then breathe in again.

4-4-6-2 Breathing

This breathing pattern is easy for children to learn and is very good at helping them to relax. It is something that they can turn to on their own when feeling anxious.

Inhale for a count of four, hold for four, exhale for a count of six, hold for two, and then repeat.

Breath-Body-Mind

Breath-Body-Mind (breath-body-mind.com) aims to increase awareness of the healing power of breath to enhance physical and mental health. There are several excellent videos and webinars on the website that introduce healthy ways of breathing, some directed at children.

Mindfulness and Meditation

Mindfulness and meditation are a huge source of learning how to be with difficult or happy emotions with an observing eye. Children—and adults—can learn that they don't need to turn away from the feelings but can let them pass through, as they inevitably do if not pushed to one side.

Five Senses

If your child seems worried or fearful or might benefit from calming down, this is an excellent tool, and one that she can learn and use to self-soothe when she feels the need.

Sit with your child and ask her what she sees around her, describing in as much detail as she can. Then move on to each of the other four senses and again ask her to describe what she hears, smells, tastes, and feels by touch. As she focuses on the here and now, she will get through the difficult moment. You can go through the senses over and over if you would both like.

Meditation

Guided meditation can offer your child a way to calm down and again is something she can add to her own toolbox of coping mechanisms once you have taught her the skills.

Here are some simple scripts to introduce your child to meditation:

o Settle yourself and feel what you are sitting on, how it holds you and supports you. Gently close your eyes if you like. Imagine you are in your favorite place—one where you feel most safe and most comfortable. Think to yourself: What does it look like? What colors are there? What smells? What kind of sounds? As you picture yourself there, relax your eyes, let your mouth hang open, relax your shoulders, let your belly go soft, relax your arms, hands, legs, and feet. Notice your breathing and now let's breathe slowly together. Breathe in as I count to five, breathe out as I count to five. Let's do that together for a few minutes. (You would continue to count to five as your child breathes in and out.)

   As we get ready to return our awareness to here, let yourself know that all the relaxation you're feeling can come back with you as you leave your favorite place for now. Stretch your arms up and let's open our eyes.

o Settle yourself and feel what you are sitting on, how it holds you and supports you. Gently close your eyes if you like. Imagine your favorite color and picture it in your mind. Let's imagine that a beautiful light of that color is above you and sending soft light from the top of your head to the tips of your toes. It is a healing light and a calming light, and as it passes through you let's breathe slowly together. Breathe in as I count to five, then breathe out as I count to five. Let's do that together for a few minutes. (You would continue to count to five as your child breathes in and out.)

   As we get ready to return our awareness to here, let yourself know that all the good feelings from the beautiful light can come back with you. Stretch your arms up and let's open our eyes.

o Settle yourself and feel what you are sitting on, how it holds you and supports you. Gently close your eyes if you like and listen. (You would play a sound your child likes, such as waves, a flowing river, or a breeze in trees.) Let the sound wash over you and relax your eyes, let your mouth hang open, relax your shoulders, let your belly go soft, relax your arms, hands, legs, and feet. Notice your breathing and now let's breathe slowly together. Breathe in as I count to five, breathe out as I count to five. Let's do that together for a few minutes. (You would continue to count to five as your child breathes in and out.)

As we get ready to return our awareness to here, let yourself know that all the relaxation you're feeling can come back with you. Stretch your arms up and let's open our eyes.

There are many apps available for meditation and some provide guided meditations for children. If this interests you, we recommend you listen to several yourself and see what might work for your child. We like Insight Timer and Headspace ourselves, but a simple Internet search will provide you with plenty of options.

ACKNOWLEDGMENTS

ELENA AND MICHAEL

We wrote this book in an effort both to impart our understanding and to offer our support to those who strive to protect the well-being of the children they nurture as they face difficult times of loss. We have many people to thank for their help in bringing this book to fruition.

Lindsey Tate was an incredibly fortunate find for us as clinicians and authors. Immediately we knew that she was the one we wanted to invite on our journey to help us create this book. As the writing unfolded, we experienced her ready grasp of our message, her outstanding work ethic, her consistent reliability, and her gifted use of language. It could not have been easy working with two people—close colleagues and friends, but with their own backgrounds and styles—to make one manuscript so respectful of both of us. Somehow, she did that and more, and we are very grateful for the essential synergy she provided. We are thankful to Terry Benes for her prescient introduction.

We hit the jackpot with Esther Newberg and Kristyn Keene Benton and the team at ICM Partners. They have been more responsive and available than we dared hope. As our agents, as well as our unstinting advocates whose guidance we respect and whose Zoom conversations and consultations we relish, they provided the engine that made the publication of this book possible. We are forever indebted to them for making our hopes a reality. We are appreciative of Holli and Ben Sax for their kind introduction at the outset that afforded us the opportunity to present our book proposal directly, and led to such a happy match.

Hannah Steigmeyer has been our dream editor, discerning yet deeply respectful of our work. Lindsey joins us in appreciating her direction that helped us to fine-tune the manuscript and ensure readers would hear our message clearly. She and the team at Avery, with Megan Newman at the helm, were thoughtful, accessible, and collaborative throughout. We are thankful for all their hard work to ensure the book's readability and to promote its dissemination.

From the moment we met her, Emi Battaglia impressed us with her straightforwardness, her knowledge, and her thoughtfulness. She has been generous with her time, been remarkably responsive, and made our public relations another way of understanding and approaching those who might read our book. We are grateful to have her with us and are better for her efforts.

ELENA

There are so many people that I want to thank for helping to make *Giving Hope* a reality.

Michael Schwartzman and I had known each other for many years when I asked him to write this book with me. I thought quite carefully about that choice, knowing how well we would have to be able to work together, how shared our perspectives would have to be, and how much time we would be spending in each others' lives. I was thrilled when he agreed. I already held him in esteem, having seen the benefit of his work with parents and children in schools. I already knew that we shared being with people's pain and suffering with openness and respect. As we began working on this book together, I learned that he was an excellent collaborator. I looked forward to our hours of writing and sharing ideas. We talked and talked—and talked some more—embodying the belief in the value of conversation that is so central to what we purport in these pages.

A lot of family members contributed to this book's passage to publication. My cousins Nathan Schachtman and Stephen Brody pitched in with their sharp legal eyes. Early in my childhood, my father, Sumner Goldstein, began a steady education in how to directly face life's dark moments, some involving death, and later even his own dying. That laid the foundation for being anchored as my life unfolded.

In order to include very personal stories of our experience with Liza's dying, I asked the people I love to bring to mind and have made public memories of times that were beyond painful when first lived through and that they carry with them in their cores. My brother-in-law and his wife, Eric and Marcie Lister, and my two amazing nieces Kalen and Johanna responded with warmth and openness to my request. My mother-in-law, Charlotte Lister, never ceased to convey her unconditional love and her certainty that I had something important to say that should be turned into a book.

The center of my life, my immediate family—Phil, Molly, Jason, and Solomon—also bravely and generously sifted through difficult memories. I could not have written this book nor be doing the work I do nor even be who I am without their unflagging sustenance. My heart is made complete by being with Phil, my husband for thirty-seven years. We cry together. We laugh even more. Molly, Jason, and Solomon galvanize me by how remarkably determined they are to be the best human beings they can be. The love and belief in me that they demonstrate every day fuels me like no other fuel on earth. And Liza, always here in memory, taught and inspired me by her resolute valor through illness and unflinching confrontation with the end of a too-short life.

I am blessed to have "friends who are family." People who know me and accept me as I am. We are there to bear witness through each other's lives, including my writing this book. My "sisters from another mother"—Martha Adler, Lorraine Anastasio, Dawn Drzal, Judy Gallent, Emily Harris, Lisa Rubin, and Dale Schomer—have been unfaltering encouragers and embody what really being there for someone means. In addition, Dawn Drzal, an editor and published author herself, generously gave wise counsel on book writing at the drop of a hat. Lisa Rubin has been on life's journey with me since we were six years old. She was a fountain of creative ideas, envisioning how our message could be sent out—doing so with such genuine enthusiasm that I couldn't help but be buoyed. Helena Thornley, MD, the palliative-care physician who took care of Liza and a friend ever since then, has been my model of compassion, strength, kindness, and steadfastness in being with people's suffering. Burt Lerner and Lois Wolf, Jules and Susan Kerman have been present with their insightful minds and loving shoulders to lean on since Liza died. Along the way, I have been perceptively guided by Gerry Fogel, Shira Ruskay, William Zangwill, Roger St. Pierre, Diane Greene, and Ben Spratt. In the past year, I have been supported and taught by the heartful people in my meditation sangha led by the sage and compassionate Barbara Newell. And I will have to allow for the other friends knowing who they are because I have only so many pages to write my acknowledgments, much as I wish I could name each one.

My patients and the people at schools, organizations, and companies where I consult have been courageously open and vulnerable, allowing me to be on their journey with them facing illness, loss, and all of life's joys and sorrows. We have been in the trenches together, collaborating to help them to cope with their challenges, and they inspire me every day. The depth of my respect and gratitude for them is enormous. May this book in some way offer them ease.

Likewise, faculty and staff at New York-Presbyterian Hospital, the Columbia Vagelos College of Physicians and Surgeons, the Columbia Center for Psychoanalytic Training and Research, and Weill Cornell

Medical College and Medical Center—my home bases since my days as a medical student—as well as other medical centers and universities across the country have opened their doors (and their hearts), offering me opportunities to share all that I have understood from the stories of grief and hope I am privileged to be with every day. Medical students and residents, supervisees and medical faculty have listened, discussed ideas, and even bravely shared their own stories of grief as together we have learned to bear the unbearable. We do this so that they can then do so with their patients. You may not know it but you have each made an indelible imprint on me.

Several organizations that I deeply respect and am inspired by have allowed me to participate in the work they do. It does not do justice to list them here but the people there know in more depth how much I feel that the world is a better place because of their efforts. They include Camp Erin and COPE Foundation, Reimagine, Rethink the Conversation, Courageous Parents Network, the Shira Ruskay Center, the Cameron Kravitt Foundation, and the Visiting Nurse Service. Thankfully there are now national organizations that I am connected with that are devoted to helping children and families cope with loss: the Association for Death Education and Counseling, the National Alliance for Children's Grief, and the National Hospice and Palliative Care Organization, to name a few.

My family's journey through Liza's illness and death has shaped my work and my very being since it began. It engendered emotional pain beyond what I thought myself capable of enduring and yet out of it grew an even deeper appreciation for all the moments we are alive, be they easy or hard, happy or sad. I wanted to write this book to help others facing loss, to hopefully bring to them all that I learned as I traversed this most painful part of my life so that they would not have to feel emotionally alone on their own journeys. The experience of actually bringing *Giving Hope* to fruition resonates with our message: as we move forward, alongside the agony of loss, it is possible to discover productivity, growth, grit, and, dare I say it, even pleasure.

My heart goes out to all of you. Take care.

MICHAEL

I have had the advantage of working with many wonderful people during a career that now spans more than four decades. My contribution to this book stems first from my close work with my patients, who have shared with me their most personal thoughts and feelings, fears and wishes. Without their willingness to examine and give voice to their own inner lives, this book would not have been possible. For their trust and generosity with me, I am respectfully grateful. Ongoing conversations and challenging questions with family and friends have created a fertile environment where my own reactions and ideas about my clinical work have been free to germinate and grow. Observations, formulations, and refinements have come from colleagues and mentors and I am thankful for their insights and the understandings our exchanges have provided me through the years. My gratitude for all these privileged relationships remains a mainstay of my work, reminding me of the critical importance of nurturing connections in our lives.

Forever on my mind and orienting me in my clinical thinking are my teachers who shared their wisdom as well as deep knowledge with me, Dr. Nathan Stockhamer, Diana Siskind, CSW, and Dr. Anni Bergman. Especially important professional colleagues who have become my dear friends, Dr. Allan Cassorla, Dr. Jonathan Cohen, and Dr. Bryant Welch, have been particularly supportive during this time. Rabbi Jeffrey Sirkman, my friend for over thirty years with whom I have shared deep losses, has provided solace and a living model for moving forward and embracing life after loss. Shepherd Morrow, one of my oldest friends from childhood, has offered much-appreciated guidance and support about the intricacies of bringing a book to fruition. Walks with my close friend Steven Roberts provided me with thoughtful conversation and valuable support. I am grateful to all of you and cherish my relationships with each one of you.

This book was first conceived by Dr. Elena Lister, who enlisted me to share in writing a guide for parents about talking with children about illness, death, and loss. Elena has the capacity to listen to everything with exceptional warmth, calmness, and empathy, and it is in this spirit that we have endeavored to share what we have learned with our readers. Not effortless, our collaboration was of the very best kind—challenging, inquisitive, always urging each other to our very best work—and I am beyond grateful to her for inviting me to join her in this endeavor. With her I have found a rewarding and productive creative partnership, an unparalleled addition to my professional life.

My work in schools has been critical to me both in being able to observe firsthand so many child and family interactions and also through the many ongoing conversations I have had with students, their parents, and educators. I am deeply appreciative of Head of School David Trower and the Allen-Stevenson School community. For almost thirty years, they have provided me an extraordinary collaboration. I thank Kim Kyte, Anne Meyer, Susan Etess, Neal Kamsler, Steve Warner, Steve Cohen, Ben Neulander, Michelle Demko, Jennifer Vermont-Davis, Chris Acerbo, and Daryl Shapiro for the closeness we share. I also am profoundly indebted to Headmaster David O'Halloran and the Saint David's School for their openness and for our innovative work together that has been so meaningful to me over the past nineteen years. Kim Davidson, Aly Aoyama, Val Suslak, Chris Guba, Esther Formosa, Kathryn Hunter, Evan Morse, David May, Jack Sproule, Pedro Morales, Allison Vella, and Sara Peavy have been outstanding partners. In both of these educational communities, we have proudly created psychologically informed programs that have served our students and their families in unique and comprehensive ways.

Most recently, the newly created, self-named "super squad," an informal group of professional psychologists who work in the New York City private boys' schools, has offered unique perspectives. Dedicated to helping to raise a cohort of resilient, empathic, self-aware, and moral young men, the group and its support, shared experiences, and good humor have been of immeasurable value to me as I grappled with some of the difficult content of this book.

Finally, there are the people I come from, with whom I have shared life, joy, and grief. First, my parents, grandparents, and in-laws, who laid the foundation for all that follows. I am thankful for my brothers and their families and the lives we share together. As always, I am guided and humbled by my love for my children, Joey, Adam, and Lianna, who have shown me that no conversation is the last. As with everything I do, so with this book. I have been lovingly supported by my wife and fellow psychologist, Dr. Lisa Weiss. Without her, I would be incapable of what I do here. I love you, Lisa.

LINDSEY

When Elena and Michael approached me about working with them on a book to help young children understand and talk about death, I immediately sensed the importance of the project. It felt close to many things I value: acknowledging and managing difficult feelings, the power of conversation, the way that honesty with children reaps its own rewards. It was only as we worked on the book, meeting and discussing on weekly Zooms as the world beyond our screens darkened and we all struggled through a global pandemic, that I truly began to understand the beauty in Michael and Elena's words and the compassion of their vision. I'm grateful that they trusted me to bring their lifelong work into being in book form. I'm especially glad that when terminal illness and death encroached on my own life that they supported me and held me close. Work on the book gave me a much-needed sense of structure and their words, transformed into wisdom throughout *Giving Hope*, helped me through an excruciating time.

Thanks and much gratitude and love are owed to my family: to James, Sophie, and Antonia, who limited their own streaming sessions when it was time for my multiple Zoom calls and remained (mostly) patient with my strict work schedule. They were deeply kind as I grieved even while undergoing struggles and sadness of their own.

INDEX

J

journals, writing or drawing in,
118, 133

L

language choices for discussing
death
addressing loss of loved ones,
232–33
avoiding euphemisms, 74
and death by suicide, 173, 176,
212, 214
and death of a child's sibling, 211
and death of a parent, 207
and death of an unborn child,
217, 218
and pets with terminal illnesses,
164, 165
lies about death
about pets' deaths, 40–42
as breach of trust, 86
having a conversation to correct,
61–62
importance of avoiding, 81–82
life after death, 57, 61–63, 78, 93
life cycle, children's awareness of,
27–28, 52–53, 56
lifespans in modern world, 20
life-threatening illnesses, 150
listening, attentive, 106–7
literalism of children, 62, 153
"lost" euphemism for death,
avoiding, 74

M

magical/wishful thinking
and avoidance of death, 56, 57
and self-blame of children, 99–100
and terminal illnesses, 152–53
mastery, children's sense of, 161–62
media coverage of tragic events,
185–200

breaking news of a tragedy, 190–91
and causes of tragedies, 196–98
children's awareness of, 26, 186,
190
clarifying your message about, 189
and combating feelings of
helplessness, 198–99
and coping mechanisms, 199–200
as daily occurrence, 186
emotional responses to, 198
encouraging perspective on, 195
and fears for safety, 194–96
focusing on positive outcomes
from, 192, 197
limiting access to, 193
questions about, 191, 193–98
reactions of children to, 191–92
and self-awareness of parents,
187–89
telling the truth about, 187, 191,
194, 196–97
medical advances and modern
longevity, 20
memorials for the dead
for a beloved teacher, 24
for pets that have died, 167
resources for, 242
memories, creating, 141
mindfulness and meditation, 231,
251, 252–54
miscarriages and stillbirths
conversations about, 216–18
disenfranchised grief following,
142–43
grieving as a family, 50
and managing emotions, 45–47
and omission of unnecessary
details, 94–95
organizations helping families
with, 242
misunderstandings about death, 30
Moana (film), 60–61, 63